Other Prompted Visions

Short stories by

P R Ellis

ellifont

Other Prompted Visions
Short stories by P R Ellis

First published in Great Britain by ellifont, 2023

ellifont
www.ellifont.wordpress.com
prelliswriter@btinternet.com

ISBN 978-1-8381935-6-0

Designed and formatted by ellifont

Other books

by Peter R Ellis
(published by Elsewhen)

The Evil Above the Stars trilogy:
Seventh Child
Power of Seven
Unity of Seven

Cold Fire

An Extraordinary Tale

by P R Ellis
(published by ellifont)

The Jasmine Frame Detective series:
Painted Ladies
Bodies By Design
The Bride's Club Murder
Molly's Boudoir
Impersonator

e-book novellas/collections:
Discovering Jasmine,
Murder In Doubt,
Trained By Murder

Anthologies

Prompted Visions: SF & F stories for writing groups

Other Prompted Visions – short stories

Title	Page
Preface	1
<u>Historical Fiction</u>	2
And there was light	3
Thicker than water	7
Keeping the flame	12
Seed	16
The Great Outdoors	20
This Time of Trial	23
Report from the Home Front	27
Fallen Apples	32
Forces' Sweetheart	36
<u>The Others</u>	38
Cup of tea	39
Reunion	42
Shoes	45
The Necessity of a Raincoat	48
The room at the top of the stairs	57
Snowdrops for St Dwynwen	59
The one that got away	61
Look to the future	65
Sisters	68
The Addict	72
Torch	77
All Plaided and Plumed	83
Silver Spoon	86
White Goods	89
Traffic	91
The Missing Essence	94
All the Stars in the Heavens	97

Step   99

Heels   102

A question of declination   106

Garden Party   112

Parallel Parking   117

Pretty Woman   119

The Accident   122

The Tales of Agent Kappa   123

Propelled to Glory   124

Message   130

Imposter   136

A Diet of Treachery   147

P R Ellis – a short biography   153

Acknowledgements   155

Preface

This is a companion volume to my anthology of short stories for writing groups, Prompted Visions. That was a collection of many of the science fiction and fantasy short stories I have written in the last decade or so, principally in response to prompts set by the writing clubs I belonged and belong to. This consists of the others – the historical fiction, the spy stories, and other genres that have also been written to prompts of one sort or another and have been read to or by my friends.

SF & F is perhaps my first love. Often my first thoughts when provided with a prompt is an SF or fantasy scenario, but not exclusively so. It is sometimes relaxing and stimulating to write in another genre. Nevertheless, I cannot stop science creeping to the fore so some of the stories do have some science content even though I do not consider the story to be SF.

Whatever genre they are, these stories have given me pleasure writing them and I hope each provides you, the reader, with something that makes you think. I do not expect an anthology to be read from cover to cover but to be dipped into from time to time when one has a few minutes to relax.

Enjoy.

P R Ellis
Sept. 2023

Historical Fiction

History starts yesterday, so I've heard. Historical fiction is work of the imagination, but it must fit in a true historical background. It can be about events that have been recorded as having occurred or just related to them. It should not contain elements of fantasy such as magic, other than a true historical response to such issues. The stories that follow do I think follow those principles.

And There Was Light – Introduction

The theme presented to writing club was "orange". As well as being one of my favourite colours it also brought to mind the history of the colour. The History of Science is one of my interests and Newton's seven colours of the spectrum a pet topic of mine. The event I describe is solely my imagination although Joseph did exist as a childhood friend and assistant of Isaac Newton so perhaps something like it did happen.

And There Was Light

The room was dark when Master Isaac closed the door behind us. Thick curtains covered the glazed window. Why anyone should do that on such a sunny summer's day, I could not understand.

"Just stand for a few moments, Joseph, and let your eyes adjust," Isaac said. "You always had clear eyesight. That's why I asked for you to join me today."

Isaac and I had played together as children although I hesitate to say we were friends. He was always somewhat alone with his thoughts. He went off to the Grammar School and then university while I was set to work on the farm. He was only home now because of the fear of plague sweeping through the towns. Perhaps it was the lack of debate with his fellow scholars that caused him to seek my company.

Gradually my eyes became accustomed to the dimness. There was Isaac standing on the other side of the table on which there was a stand. On it I could make out a rod of glass with a triangular cross section.

"I don't want you to look at the prism, Joseph. Focus your eyes on the wall opposite the window." The wall was featureless but even in the absence of almost all light I could see that it had been given a fresh coat of limewash.

Isaac moved behind me and, in the darkness, there was. . .light! A rainbow appeared on the white wall. Well, not the curve of a bow. The colours were in the shape of a somewhat distorted rectangle. I turned and saw there was a tiny hole in the curtain through which a beam of sunlight passed and fell on the prism. Out of the glass came a shaft of colour that projected onto the wall.

"What have you done, Master Isaac?" I said with some awe in my voice.

"I have proved that white light is not, as the ancients thought, a single entity, but a blending of light of various colours. The prism disperses the colours so that they can be seen side by side. But that is by the by. What I want you to do is tell me what colours you can see. Step close and examine the pattern the light makes."

I did as bidden and leaned close to the wall.

"What do you see, Joseph?"

"I see red and green and blue." I replied.

"Yes, but I want more than that. What do you see between the red and the green?"

Fixing my eyes on that area of the image I saw that the colours went through a multitude of variations.

"The red becomes yellowish," I said, "then the yellow loses the reddish hue and tends towards the green."

"Ah, yes, the yellowish red and the reddish yellow. Do you not have a name for that, Joseph?"

He could not see me shake my head in the shadows. "No, Master Isaac," I said.

"It is orange, is it not?"

Orange. The word was strange but not unknown to me, though I had little understanding of what it meant.

"What is orange?" I asked.

"Have you not seen an orange? No, of course you haven't, Joseph. You have never even been to Grantham have you." He paused for a breath. "An orange is a fruit. Its peel has a texture like that of a lemon, but its flesh is much sweeter and pleasant on the tongue. The name of the colour is derived from that of the fruit because its skin is that particular hue. So, do you see a band of orange between that of the red and the yellow.

I was not sure I saw bands, but rather a gradation of colours, nevertheless I thought it wise to agree with Isaac.

"Now what do you see at the other end, after the green?" he asked.

"I see blue." In fact, I saw a variety of shades of blue.

"Don't you see violet at the end of the spectrum?" Isaac stabbed the wall where the blue dimmed to darkness."

"I suppose that could be called violet," I acknowledged.

"And do you not see indigo?"

"Indigo?" I was confused, "you mean the dye?"

"That's correct, and also the name for its colour."

"But the dye is blue, Master Isaac."

"A distinctive shade of blue. Is it not there between the blue and the violet." He pointed to the part of the rainbow he was referring to."

The colours faded and disappeared. We were cast into gloom once more. Isaac stomped across the floor and threw back the curtains. Heavy clouds had obscured the Sun. It looked as if it might rain.

"It seems our opportunity for experiment is over," Isaac said. He picked up a sheet of paper and put it on the table in front of me. "Don't you think this describes what we have seen."

The paper had several lines ruled in ink across it and between the lines there was writing. I picked out the letters till the words came to me, from top to bottom – red, orange, yellow, green, blue, indigo, violet.

"Surely you saw those bands of coloured light in the rainbow, Joseph."

"Only the seven?" I queried, thinking of how the colours had appeared to me in endless variation.

"Of course, seven, Joseph," Isaac replied, somewhat sharply. "Seven, as in the days of the week and the metals known to antiquity. Seven, as in the notes of the musical scale. In the same way that our ears are sensitive to the distinctive notes of the octave, so our eyes see the seven colours of the rainbow. Seven, as in the wanderers in the heavens." He fell to muttering and moved across the room, turning the pages of a book on the lectern and then taking up his pen to scribble on a sheet of paper. I realised that I had faded from his attention as quickly as the rainbow had disappeared from the wall.

Soon, with the passing of the plague, Isaac returned to Cambridge. We never spoke again. He became a professor and I heard that he was lauded by the learned men of London. I knew nothing of his work but whenever I saw a rainbow in the sky, I recalled my participation in his experiment. Sometimes I felt I could even see the seven bands of colour that he insisted on. I could usually pick out the orange. Later I held an orange fruit. It was as Isaac described. Orange became a popular colour when William of the House of Orange was crowned King in place of the papist, James. Yes, I believe in orange, but indigo? I confess, I cannot tell where amongst the blue, indigo is supposed to fit but if the famous philosopher Isaac Newton says it is there, it must be so.

Thicker than water – Introduction

"Blood relations" was the suggested theme for this piece. It got me thinking about blood transfusions and I did some digging. The story of the American-led incursion into northern Russia following the October revolution of 1917 is little known. The story is fiction though something similar apparently did happen.

Thicker than water

"How's the Major doing, Doc?" Captain Madison said, ducking under the flap at the entrance to the treatment tent.

The blast of cold air caused Medical Officer Jackson to look up from his sewing. "I've done all I can for him, Captain, but he's lost a lot of blood."

"He's going to live, isn't he?" Madison said, his voice trembling.

Jackson shrugged. "Touch and go."

"We're going to have to move camp very soon," the Captain muttered, "The Bolsheviks are advancing."

Jackson sucked through his teeth. "Unless Major Coolidge shows some improvement, moving him is not going to do him any good at all."

Captain Madison stepped towards the portable operating table cradling his bandaged frostbitten left hand. "Is there nothing more you can do?"

The doctor considered his reply. "Perhaps. He needs a blood transfusion."

"A what?"

"An injection of fresh blood to replace what he has lost."

"Where do you get fresh blood from?"

"One of you. Preferably a soldier who is still tolerably fit."

"Is that all?"

"No. He needs to match the Major's blood group."

Captain Madison looked blank. "How can you know that?"

Jackson gave a wry smile. "It's on every soldier's records."

"You still have the medical records?"

"Yes, Captain, despite our frequent changes of camp."

Madison's raised eyebrows showed surprise. "So, you know who matches the Major?"

"I do."

Madison's eyes search the doctor's blank face for a clue. Was it him that would be required to give blood? "That's good, isn't it. What do you have to do?"

"Call in the soldier concerned and take a pint of his blood."

The Captain's face, burnt by the arctic air turned a shade whiter. "You said, soldier. Is there only one match."

"Unfortunately, it is just one. It is Private Taylor. Normally I would request permission from both donor and recipient but that's not possible here." The doctor nodded at the comatose form of the Major.

Madison opened his mouth to reply and paused. "Er, Private Taylor is black."

The doctor nodded. "Yes, Captain, but don't worry. There is no difference between a white man's blood and black man's of the same group. The Major can accept Private Taylor's blood without ill effect."

The Captain shuffled. "But, Doc, you know the Major's opinion of blacks."

"I've heard him say a few things."

"Well, what do you think he'll say if he discovers that he's got a black man's blood in his veins."

Jackson shrugged. "It's either that or he's dead. There's no way the allied forces are going to get anyone else's blood to us while we're retreating to Archangel."

The Captain bit his lip. Various thoughts passed through his mind. At last, he spoke. "Well, I can't see that there's any choice. You'd better get on with it, Doc. I'll call Private Taylor."

Doctor Jackson examined the jar of blood then connected it to the catheter inserted in the Major's arm.

The big man with skin as black and shiny as a mahogany piano sat holding the pad of lint to his arm. "Is the Major going to be OK?"

"I hope so, Private. You've given him his best chance of recovery."

"Hmm."

The doctor felt that something needed to be said. "Look, I know the Major has said some pretty damn nasty things about people like you."

"Black citizens of the United States," Taylor said without any hint of rancour.

"That's correct Taylor. You didn't have to consent to give blood, you know."

"But he would have died without it."

"Probably."

Private Taylor straightened up and lifted his head, "Then it was my duty to help him, not just as a serving soldier but as a human being."

The doctor nodded. "That's right, Private Taylor. I hope the Major sees it the same way."

Madison gazed at the Major, hardly able to believe the change. The Major was sitting up in bed. His skin had a healthy, pink tinge.

"You're looking a lot better, Sir."

"Getting there, Captain. The doc tells me that as well as patching me up he gave me a shot of blood."

"That's right, Sir."

"Well, whose was it, Captain? Yours?"

"No, Sir. I wasn't a match though I would have been honoured to donate my blood to you if it had been."

"Then who the damn was it?"

Madison hesitated. Doctor Jackson looked up from examining the sleeping patient in the adjacent camp bed. "It was Private Taylor, Major."

"Taylor?" The Major looked blank then his face showed memory returning. "Private Taylor, the . . ."

"Black American soldier," Jackson interrupted, "Yes, Major, it was him."

Major Coolidge's cheeks puffed out, then he let the air go. "Well, the sonuvabitch. So, I've got black blood in me."

The Medical Officer replied in his no-nonsense voice. "No Major, it's the same colour red as your own, and all your brothers and sisters and fellow Americans whether they are white, black or yellow. In fact, you and Private Taylor quite possibly have a closer match in your blood than you and most of your family." He pointed to the person lying in the bed. "One pint wasn't enough for you, so I had to take more from Private Taylor. He's a strong, young man but it took a lot out of him. He's sleeping now. It'll be days before he's fully recovered."

Coolidge frowned. "You made him give me his blood, Doctor?"

"No, Major. He volunteered. He said it was his duty to the United States of America."

Coolidge thrust out his chin, swallowed, and sniffed. "So, Private Taylor and I are blood relations, are we."

The doctor half shrugged, half nodded, "You could say that, Major."

"Goddamn it, Doc, that's a curveball you've pitched me. I guess I have to thank the guy."

Keeping the Flame – Introduction

The event this story describes definitely did occur. Michael Faraday's lecture on the history of the candle is one of the most famous of the Christmas Lectures presented at the Royal Institution in London that continue to this day. As they are today, they were directed at children and there were many girls in the audience so Ellen, though a fiction, is not a fanciful character. This piece was written in response to the topic "candles".

Keeping the flame

"Stop it, Ellen. If you don't behave, I will suggest to your father that you should not attend the Royal Institution this afternoon."

Nanny's words had an immediate effect on me. I did not want to miss the journey into London, so I decided to do as she requested. I finished eating the lunch that had been placed before me and soon it was time to don clothes suitable for venturing into society.

Shortly before two p.m. I joined Father in the hallway of our home. Despite it being but the fourth day of Christmas there was no decoration. We had not celebrated the festival this year. Nanny fussed over me while Father urged us to hurry into the carriage. It was a typical December day, cold, damp, foggy and the air stank of the smoke from the coal that we and our neighbours burned in our house fires. Nanny wrapped a blanket around me for the journey. As we set off along the muddy street, I addressed Father.

"Papa, Mama said that Mr Faraday would lecture on 'The Chemical History of the Candle'."

He held up a slip of paper and peered at it. "That is indeed the title on the ticket that your Mother purchased before. . ." His voice faded away and he looked out of the window.

"How can he talk for a whole hour about candles?" I said.

"That we shall find out soon, Ellen," Nanny said, "Don't upset your father."

I was not to be diverted. "But we have gaslight in our house. Why doesn't he talk about the Chemical History of Gaslight?"

Father sighed. "I am sure Mr Faraday has a very good reasons for the title of this year's Christmas Lectures. He has been delivering them for over twenty years. I am certain that he knows what will instruct and entertain his audience."

"Will he make explosions, Papa?" I asked, eagerly.

"Let us wait and see."

It was only some two miles to Piccadilly but before we reached our destination, we joined a queue of carriages and cabs. Eventually we turned into Albermarle Street. All the traffic travelled at a very slow pace in the same direction. Father tapped his cane against the roof of the carriage. It stopped and we stepped down. Nanny took my hand as we walked the last few yards to the grand entrance of the Royal Institution. There was a crush, as many people were of the same intention.

We took our seats in the steeply banked auditorium. Below us there was a large horse-shoe-shaped table on which stood many pieces of apparatus and quite a few candles. Just one was lit. At last, the crowd hushed, and Mr Faraday entered through a door behind the table. Father had told me that he was the most famous man of science in the country, but he was quite a small, retiring man with white hair.

He began to speak and his voice filled the hall. He asked us all to look carefully at the lit candle and note that though the candlewax was the fuel that fed the flame, it was solid and upright.

For the next hour I was mesmerised by Mr Faraday's talk. He explained the principles by which a candle gives out light so clearly and entertainingly and his demonstrations illustrated the points that he made so appropriately that I felt that, despite being of few years, I understood all that he had said. I was filled with enthusiasm for science and talked of nothing else on the dark journey home. As we stepped down from our carriage I spoke to Father.

"May I try out Mr. Faraday's experiments, Papa?"

"I am sure that is possible, my dear. Nanny will supervise you but take care with the candle flame."

"Yes, Papa."

I noticed that there was a tear in his eye, as I left him. I took Nanny's hand and dragged her to the school room. She brought a candle from her room, and holding a taper to the gaslight, transferred the flame to the wick. I observed it closely as instructed by Mr Faraday and saw the little pool of liquid wax that formed just below the flame.

"I wish Mama was here," I said.

"I am sure she is, in spirit," Nanny replied.

"She would help me do Mr Faraday's experiments, wouldn't she?"

"Yes, Ellen," Nanny's voice wavered, "She would be pleased to see you taking up science. She was an admirer of Mr Faraday for many years and often expressed the wish that she could be a scientist too."

"Why couldn't she be a scientist?" I asked.

Nanny sniffed. "It is said, by men, that only men have the intellectual capacity to pursue scientific knowledge."

"Then I will become one for Mama."

The candle flame flickered as if in response to my resolution.

Seed – Introduction

Another tale of scientific discovery. Perhaps it occurred as I describe, perhaps not, but the discovery was made in something like this fashion. The topic provided by writing group was "seed" but I don't think the seed I had in mind was the general idea.

Seed

My master hurried down the stairs towards me, his linen shirt but roughly tucked into his breeches. He carried a small wooden spoon carefully in two hands.

"Ah, Johan," he said, gasping for breath, "Open the door to my study."

I did his bidding and held the door while he passed me. I was about to close the door behind him but he called out again.

"No, boy, join me. I have an observation to make which may be of interest to you." I stepped inside the wood-panelled room, brightly lit by the sun which shone through the many small panes of the large, glazed window. I closed the door behind me and stood beside my master's table.

He dipped a small silver spatula into the glutinous liquid on the spoon that he had so carefully carried down the stairs. Then he picked up one of the instruments that lay on the desk and, peering closely at it, transferred the tiniest globule of the fluid to the tip of the pin. I was unable to see if he was successful, but he let out a held-in breath.

"Yes," he muttered, "that should be satisfactory."

He turned to face the window and held the instrument to his left eye. He stood like a statue for many heartbeats. Having witnessed this procedure many times and indeed having carried it out myself I knew he was observing something of interest.

Eventually he moaned. "Magnificent." He moved the instrument away from his face and blinked a few times.

I was filled with curiosity. "What have you seen Master Leeuvenhoek? What is the fluid that you have examined?"

He looked at me as if debating whether to answer, then he made up his mind.

"I have lain with my wife," he said in a soft, calm voice.

I consider myself to be of some intelligence but it took me a few moments to understand what he meant. When I did, I felt a blush rise from my neck and fill my cheeks.

I spoke but could not fully enunciate the words, "The fluid is . . ."

"My seminal ejaculation. Yes, Johan," he answered as if it was the most normal subject of conversation. "That which may cause a woman to be with child."

"What did you see, Master?" I asked, my eagerness for knowledge surpassing my embarrassment.

He held out the instrument to me. "See for yourself."

I took the small bronze item from him. It was no bigger than my finger and consisted of a flat plate in which there was a tiny hole. Behind the plate was a system of rods and screws which moved the pin on which the drop of fluid resided. I too turned to face the sunlight and held the microscope to my eye. The metal plate almost touched the surface of my eyeball. Within the hole was a tiny glass sphere barely bigger than a mustard seed. The bright beam of sunlight passed through the drop of semen, through the glass bead and into my eye.

I entered a mysterious world where what is normally too small to be seen by the human eye is miraculously enlarged. Previously Master Leeuwenhoek's instruments had revealed my hairs become as thick as tree trunks and mites grown the size of elephants. He had also shown me the strange animalcules of many different forms present in water drawn from various sources. Now I saw strange new creatures. In some respect, they resembled tadpoles. They had bulbous heads and long thin tails. Most of the creatures were motionless but some lashed their tails from side to side and thereby propelled themselves through the seminal fluid.

I moved the instrument away from my eye and breathed.

"Is this what you saw?" Master Leeuwenhoek said.

I looked down at his desk. While I had been observing he had been sketching on a sheet of letter paper. I saw an image which closely resembled the creatures I had seen through the glass.

"Yes, that is a true likeness," I said, 'What are these creatures that inhabit your effusion?"

"I believe they are the seeds of mankind," Master Leeuwenhoek said. "During coitus they are deposited within the vagina. Their propulsive efforts carry them into the womb where they take root and are nurtured to become a foetus and later a child."

"But in that tiny drop I saw many such creatures," I said, "Are all required to render the female pregnant."

Leeuwenhoek looked grave. "I fear not Johan. I think just one of these animalcules is necessary for procreation. I fancy that in the heads of some I could make out the form of a human child. Of the multitude released at the moment of orgasm only the strongest, the most deserving of God's bountiful care will result in the development of a child. That is why God insists that men should reserve their ejaculate for the procreation of children and should not waste it in pleasures of the flesh."

I felt my cheeks blush again and could find no reply. My master's vision was keener than my own despite his extra years. It was not unusual for him to have a clearer sight into the miniscule world than me.

Master Leeuwenhoek placed another sheet of paper in front of him and took up his pen. "I think I must write another letter to Mr Oldenburg, in London. I am sure he will be keen to disseminate our observations to the fellows of the Royal Society."

Anton von Leeuwenhoek's report on the discovery of spermatozoa was published in the *Philosophical Transactions* of the Royal Society of London during 1677. Unlike most of his letters which were translated from Dutch into English, this letter was translated into Latin because of its controversial topic.

The Great Outdoors - Introduction

This tale of the first spacewalk on 18th March 1965 (my birthday) is true in all details. I have just imagined what Alexei Leonov's thoughts might have been. The title suggested by my writing group was "The Great Outdoors". What could be more "outdoors" than space?

The Great Outdoors

The outer hatch swung open and Alexei floated out. No, not floated. Floating implied a fluid, water or air, to provide buoyancy. Here he was surrounded by nothing. Nothing! A tug on his tether set him rotating slowly. He looked out on darkness, the black of space. There was nothing between him and the edge of the universe but stars. Not that he could see the stars. The filters in his visor, intended to prevent his eyes from being dazzled by the Sun, rendered the stars invisible. Still, he could experience the vastness of space which was impossible inside the cramped Voskhod craft with its tiny window.

He felt motionless. He turned a bit more and the Voskhod 2 came into his field of view, itself appearing to hang stationary in the nothing. Intellectually, he knew he was falling at sixteen thousand miles per hour, but this was nothing like skydiving. There was no air to push against his suit and he, like the space capsule, was in orbit. As he turned further, the great bright globe of the Earth came into view. Beneath the brilliant whiteness of the clouds, he could make out the coast of the Mediterranean Sea, the Black Sea and across the Soviet Union, the Caspian Sea. They were just starting their second orbit, passing a little south of their launch site, Baikonur.

Pavel's voice came over the radio from inside the craft. "It's time to come back in, Alexei."

Had ten minutes passed already? He was reluctant to give up his unique view of the expanse of space. There was at least another half hour of air in his backpack, but he knew he needed to keep a good safety margin and their orbit would soon take them into the freezing cold of night. There were things to do as well as get back inside. He must take some photos of the Voskhod in space.

There was a problem. He couldn't bend or move his limbs sufficiently to operate the camera on his chest. He knew what had happened. With a vacuum outside his spacesuit, the air inside had caused it to expand like a balloon. It had become rigid. The photos didn't matter, a bigger worry was getting back into the airlock which was only just over a metre in diameter. He was supposed to go in feet first, but he could not move his legs and arms sufficiently to manoeuvre himself into the correct position. He must go in headfirst. The expanded space suit jammed in the airlock. He couldn't turn to close the outer hatch.

There was only one solution, but it was a risky one. He could just reach the valve that would let air out of the suit. That was not supposed to be done in the vacuum of space. The drop in pressure would be like a diver rising too fast from the depths. Alexei may suffer the bends and lack of oxygen to his brain could cause him to black out. Nevertheless, he had to try.

Air vented into space until he was able to twist around. It was a struggle and many minutes passed but at last he pulled the hatch closed and locked it. Only then could Pavel fill the airlock with air and open the inner hatch. Overheated and drenched in sweat, Alexei Leonov finally pulled himself back into his seat beside Pavel Belyayev. They had another

21

day and sixteen orbits to complete and a landing to achieve, but that was another nightmarish story.

This Time of Trial - Introduction

The marking of the centenary of the First World War created many opportunities for writing, a number of which follow. This one was done close to the date 100 years after the start of the war. It is a totally fictional scene, but I think we had the newspapers of the time to prompt our writing.

This Time of Trial

I was cutting flowers in the front garden when I heard that war was declared. There had been a shower earlier in the morning, but the sun was shining now. I had my arms full with iris, freesia and gladioli when I saw Ivy Broad hurrying along the pavement towards me. She was waving a newspaper. By the time she reached our front gate she was quite out of breath but still eager to give me the news,

"Dorothy," she panted, "We're at war."

A strange mixture of emotions passed through me in the moments following Ivy's announcement. First it was shock. Despite all the talk since that Austrian prince was shot, it was still a surprise to find that we were actually at war. Next, I felt pride. Our navy and army would soon put those silly Germans in their place. Then I was worried. People die in war. My own brother died in the South African war a dozen years ago or more. Our soldiers and sailors would be putting themselves in danger and no doubt some would perish in this new conflict.

"Is that the Daily Mirror you have there, Ivy?" I asked. Ivy Broad looked at the paper in her hand almost as if she had forgotten it was anything other than a fan to cool her red and perspiring face.

"Why yes, it is Dorothy."

23

"May I have a look? It may be some hours before I get a look at George's Times."

"I wonder if Mr Able was able to get one," Ivy said, "There was such a crowd at the newsagent I was very lucky to get my hands on my Mirror. My Bert will want to see it, but you can have a quick look."

Ivy handed the newspaper to me. I quickly flicked passed the first two pages of inconsequential gossip until I got to the main news. Great Britain had declared war on Germany at 11 o'clock last night and the King had sent a message to the Navy. There were also reports of the crowds who had gathered outside Buckingham Place during the evening that cheered the King and his family when they made an appearance on the balcony. The King had received a telegram from Prince Albert on his ship saying that he looked forward to Great Britain fulfilling its obligation to Belgium. There were lots of other items, but I had seen enough.

I folded the paper and handed it back to Ivy.

"Thank you, Ivy. Take it home to Mr Broad."

"People are saying we'll soon have the Germans beat, what with them up against the French and Russians as well as our brave lads. It'll be over by Christmas."

I could not emulate Ivy's confidence. It seemed to me that war was an unpredictable venture and that many people suffered from its effects.

"I very much hope so, Ivy. Now I really must get these flowers into water."

I left Ivy to continue her journey home and retired into the house.

I kept myself busy for the hours before George and Neville came home from the bank. I cut and arranged the flowers I had picked, continued with my sewing and prepared the evening meal. Neville rushed in ahead of George, keen to inform me of the news. George followed brandishing his Times and confirming Ivy's description of the crowds pushing and shoving to get their copies.

George was sombre. He rarely described his days managing the bank but today he did offer a comment.

"War is an expensive business, Dorothy," he said as he settled into his seat by the window. "Already Lloyd George has got Parliament to agree to one hundred million pounds of expenditure. Prices will rise. I am sure even you will notice the changes when you embark on your shopping expeditions."

As I visited the shops most days, I was quite sure that I would notice any increase in prices.

"When will fighting start?" I asked.

"Start? It's already started," George replied, "The Germans have invaded Belgium and are fighting both the French and Russians. Our expeditionary force will be across the English Channel before the week is out and the Navy will be seeking German targets at this moment. I tell you, soon the whole of Europe, perhaps even the whole world will be at war."

We ate our supper quietly. I tried to speak of everyday topics like Neville's part in the cricket match that had taken place on Bank Holiday Monday. It was only the day before yesterday, but it seemed a different era. George's thoughts were on the future of the bank and Neville's on the exploits of the Navy. We didn't talk much.

While I was washing up, George went pottering in the garden and Neville took the opportunity to turn the pages of the Times. I was hanging up the tea towel when Neville rushed into the kitchen with a page of the newspaper waving from his hands.

"Look at this Ma. They're inviting motorcycle riders to join the army – they're offering 35 shillings a week." Neville had got a motorcycle shortly after he joined his father working in the bank. A noisy, smelly machine it was, which seemed to spend more time in pieces than roaring along the road. It worried me when I saw him riding the thing at speeds of nearly thirty miles per hour, but he was so proud of it.

"You're not thinking of joining are you, Neville? What about the bank?"

"Oh, it won't be for long, Ma. It says it's for a year or however long the war lasts. Well, everyone knows it will be over before the year's out, so I wouldn't be away from the bank for long."

"But there will be fighting, Neville. You could get hurt."

"Oh, as a motorcyclist I'll be carrying messages. I won't be close to the shooting. Anyway, once the Huns see the British army facing them, they'll be out of Belgium as fast as lightning."

"But you have an important job, Neville. Other men can enlist."

"The King expects the whole Empire to stand united at this time of trial, Ma. It says so in the newspaper. That means everyone must do their bit. I have a motorcycle so I shall enlist."

I had to turn away from Neville then as I felt a tear in my eye. Was it pride I felt or fear? I noticed that a flower I had picked earlier and placed in a pot on the windowsill was already wilting, its head hanging down and petals dropping off. I had cut it and ended its life. How many other lives would be cut down in the days to come?

Report from the Home Front – Introduction

This too was written shortly after the centenary of the start of WW1. It covers a similar period to the previous story but from a different angle, predicting some of the changes that occurred during the conflict. While it is fictional it was based on actual newspaper reports.

Report from the Home Front

The Editor called me into his office this morning. He hasn't spoken to me directly before.

"Now, boy," he said, "I'm going to give you a chance to make a name for yourself on the Courier."

"You want me to do a report, Sir?" I asked. It was what I wanted since I'd been taken on as office-boy.

"That's right, boy," he said.

"What about Mr Smith and Mr Roberts?' I asked. They were the two reporters for the Courier.

"Smith has joined up and Roberts is following the war news. I need you to report to me on how the town is contributing to the war effort."

"The town, Sir? But the war is across the channel. The Kaiser has invaded Belgium. The Germans aren't coming here are they, Sir?"

"Of course not, boy. The fighting may be on the continent but everyone in this country is going to be involved, mark my words."

"My Mam says it'll be over by Christmas. Our soldiers will teach the Huns a lesson."

"I've heard that too, but didn't you read Sir Edward Grey's speech. 'The lamps are going out over Europe, and we shall not see them lit again in our lifetimes'. That's what he said. I fear we're in for a long haul." The Editor's gloomy prediction made me tremble.

"Oh, dear, Sir. What should I do?"

"What you are told, boy. Get out into town with your notebook and write down what you see and hear. Go!"

So that is how I found myself walking down the High Street with my cap on and notebook and pencil in my hands. It was a bright day yesterday when the declaration of war was made but today was dull. I noticed a queue of women outside the Cooperative establishment. I stopped a woman emerging with a full basket.

"Why is there a queue?" I asked. The woman looked at me in surprise.

"Because everyone wants to stock up of course. Haven't you heard there's a war on?"

"Of course, but the war isn't here."

"Who knows where it will be, but God provides for those who are prepared." She pointed to her basket. "Mind you they only let me have seven pounds of sugar, and it was four pence a pound. How I am supposed to make my jam with just seven pounds. And bacon has gone up to one and six. I've got three grown lads to feed. They say they're going to join up. Good, I say. Fight for the King and the army will feed you." She pushed past me and strode off up the street with her heavy load over her arm. I jotted her words down and then followed her.

When I got to the fire station there were about a dozen firemen parading outside in their best uniforms. I stood next to an old man leaning on a stick.

"Why are they on parade?" I asked.

"They're off to fight the Bosch," he said.

"All of them?"

"Yes. They say half the crew have been called up. They're all in the reserve yeomanry." I watched as the senior fire officer moved along the line speaking to each man while they stood stiffly to attention. I wondered what would happen if we had a fire in the town with only half the firemen left. Perhaps they would ask for volunteers. After a few moments admiring the firemen, I moved on.

There was queue at the tram and omnibus stop which was unusual for this time of a morning. A young woman carrying a laundry bag was at the end of the queue.

"Is there a problem?" I asked.

"People say that there aren't so many running today. It's really annoying. My Ma is waiting for me to bring my ironing," she said.

"Why aren't the omnibuses running?'

"The army have taken all the buses and the drivers have gone and joined up. There's hardly any left to drive the trams."

"What is the Corporation going to do?" I asked not expecting an answer. "People rely on the trams."

"They'll have to find some new drivers, won't they? Perhaps they'll let women drive. I'd love to be a tram driver."

"Women driving trams!" I was quite astonished at her suggestion and continued up the street shaking my head in disbelief. I reached the Courthouse and, glancing at the clock outside, realised that the Police Court would be in session. A seat in the public gallery would be a welcome break and allow me to jot down my notes. As I settled onto the bench two young men were led into the court by an army sergeant. They were tidily dressed in woollen jackets with caps in their hands. The magistrate, the Reverend Bellingham, leaned forward to speak to the Sergeant.

"Only two, Sergeant."

"At this time, Your Honour. I sent off a large number yesterday. I'm sure there will be plenty more willing fellows later." Rev. Bellingham nodded and read out the oath which the two men recited back in firm voices. The Recruiting Sergeant paraded the men out calling, left, right, left, right.

Two men were then led into the dock. They looked somewhat dishevelled and the worse for wear having presumably spent the night in the cells. Rev. Bellingham frowned at them.

"You are accused of being drunk and incapable," he said gravely. "What do you have to say for yourselves?"

The man who seemed to be the elder of the two, spoke up. "We're sorry m'lud. Harry 'ere, me bruvver, has been called up to fight the Hun, and we had a drop to send him off."

"Is this true, Harry Williams? You have received the call to serve His Majesty?"

The younger man nodded and held his head in shame. "Yes, m'lud," he muttered.

Rev Bellingham hammered his gavel and announced, "The case against Harry Williams is dismissed. I trust you will not bring disgrace on your country." The young man lifted his head and nodded vigorously. The Reverend continued, "Walter Williams you will pay a fine of two shillings and sixpence. I suggest you think about following the example of your brother." The Reverend stood up and swept out of the chamber.

I left the Court and re-traced my steps back to the offices of the Courier. The Editor called me to his office again.

"Well, boy, what did you find out?"

"Many men are being called up and are joining the army, Sir."

"Of course. The army currently has only two hundred thousand men while Germany alone has over a million armed and ready. Many more King's men will be needed to achieve victory."

"Should I join up, Sir," I said, feeling a sudden surge of duty.

"That is for you to decide, boy, but I can't run a newspaper without reporters."

"Perhaps women would work on the paper, Sir, and drive trams and put out fires."

"Women!" He twisted the hairs of his moustache as he pondered. "Perhaps you are right, boy. The men go to fight while the women stay and run the commerce and industry. A new world for certain."

Fallen Apples - Introduction

For this task we were given the first and last phrases but again it was during the period when the commemoration of the Great War was at the forefront of our thoughts. Like the previous pieces, it is not based on any actual memoirs, but things may have been as described.

Fallen Apples

"It's not my fault," Bert said, picking up the basket and starting to re-fill it with the apples that had spilled onto the grass. I knelt beside him and began to help him.

"What's the matter, Bert?" I asked.

"Me mind keeps wandering," he said.

"Where to?"

"Belgium."

I knew what he meant. The war across the channel was on my mind too. The reports weren't good. The Germans had advanced through Belgium and into France with our boys and the French being beaten back. It had all happened so quickly since war was declared a month ago. Bert's older brother Sid had joined the army a couple of years ago and he was over there with the British Expeditionary Force. Like Bert I wondered how Sid was doing. What must it be like fighting in battle?

We both kept our thoughts to ourselves as we got on with the job of filling baskets with apples and loading them onto the cart. After a couple more hours we'd done all that we could for one day, so we walked the horse and cart back from the orchard to the farm and unloaded it into the cider barn. It was still light when Bert and I trudged home. There were some new posters on the boards outside the general stores in town.

"Look at that," Bert said, "the boys 'ave done it." The sheet that Bert pointed at reported that the Germans had been halted at the River Marne.

"They've only stopped them," I pointed out, "the war's not over." I pointed to the poster on the other board. '*Enlist now – your country needs you*' it said in bold colourful letters with a picture of Lord Kitchener pointing his finger directly at me.

"What do you think Bert? Should we join up?"

"They said the war would be over by Christmas," he replied.

"Yeah, but they're going to need more lads if they're going to push the Huns right out of France and Belgium."

"Perhaps you and me could 'elp and give Sid an 'and." Bert said, "but what about the apples. Who'll bring them all in?"

"There's other people," I said, "Your Pa wouldn't mind a bit more work and there's my sis. She'd love to earn a few coppers."

"Yeah, well I wouldn't want to see them apples left rotting on the ground."

"They won't. Let's join up tomorrow."

"Aye."

There wasn't much left of the village we'd come to defend. Every building was damaged by the bombardments from both sides as the Germans had first taken it then been forced out. Bodies in German and British uniforms and of ordinary men and women lay amongst the muddy pools. We were the reinforcements sent by General Haig to make sure that the line was held.

"What's this 'ere place called?" Bert asked as we marched up the rubble strewn street.

"Givenchy," I replied.

"Some place to spend Christmas."

'There's a few more days yet."

"I don't reckon this war is going to be over by then, do you," Bert said wistfully.

"I think someone got it wrong, Bert.'

At the edge of the village, we entered the trenches and were ordered to get out our shovels ready to do some digging of our own.

"Keep your 'eads down," the Sergeant ordered, "or the German snipers'll have you." As he spoke there was the scream of a shell over our heads followed by a deafening thud as it exploded in the remains of a house a hundred yards behind us. As we filed through the muddy corridors, we met the defenders we were relieving. Every one of them looked exhausted and over halfway to death, covered in muck and blood.

A few hours later. I knew how they felt. I too was covered in mud from shovelling and there was plenty of blood too from the bodies of the soldiers we carried out of the shell-damaged trenches.

"They say these 'ere trenches go all the way to the sea," Bert said as we carried one mangled corpse.

"And to Switzerland, that way," I said nodding in the opposite direction.

"Is this what war has become? Blokes rotting in holes in the ground while taking pot-shots at each other."

Voices shouted; whistles blew. "Fix bayonets" came the call. Bert and I dropped our burden and swiftly slotted our bayonets to the rifles that we'd been carrying over our backs. Our weeks of training had taught us that at least, even if we were barely prepared for the realities of war. Guns fired, and

34

I heard the bullets buzzing over our heads. More shells screamed over, exploding one after the other until the roar was continuous.

"What's happening?" Bert shouted.

"Counterattack," someone replied from nearby. We held our rifles at the ready staring up at the rim of the trench. Our own howitzers opened up and the chatter of the machine guns added to the din.

"I wish I was back in the orchard," Bert bawled at me. A wave of mud thrown up by a near-miss swamped us.

"I'm sorry, Bert," I spluttered, wiping the muck from my mouth with the wet sleeve of my uniform, "It's my fault that you enlisted."

"That's right, lad," He gave me his toothy grin, "It's yours."

Forces' Sweetheart – Introduction

Another conflict. This piece was written around the time that Vera Lynn died, and she was the prompt. It is based on a true event – she did travel all the way to Burma to entertain the troops, but, of course, the interpretation of the event is purely my imagination.

Forces' Sweetheart

My mind was foggy when Nobby burst into the tent and announced there was going to be some entertainment. I can't say I felt up to another poker circle. Snap was about all I could manage after our last patrol up the hill. I'd picked up a nick from an enemy bullet and had a touch of the fever that we all got from time to time.

"I don't want none of that. I already owe you all my pay for the next year," I said, turning over on my camp bed. I just wanted to stretch out, close my eyes and dream of a cool beer and a bath.

"Come on Sid, you'll want to see this. It's a performance."

It seemed Nobby wasn't going to let me be. "What is it? Those three gunners dressed up as the Andrews Sisters? They look good enough to kiss, but I hope they've learnt to sing now."

"Na, Sid. It ain't them. It's the lass from home. The forces' sweetheart. You know 'er."

"She sings those sentimental dirges. Leave me alone."

"Aw, come on, Sid. Everyone's going. It'll cheer you up."

"What, one girl singing to five hundred knackered tommies." But, Nobby had pricked my interest. No one else came out from home to entertain our forgotten army, so it said something for this girl to make the effort.

Nobby managed to get us in a few rows from the front, so at least we had some chance of hearing. She'd brought her own pianist with a small, battered honky tonk that had gone out of tune. They gave her a microphone connected up to the camp loudspeakers powered by a couple of truck batteries.

After the customary shouts of "ger off" when the CO made his welcoming speech, she stepped onto the makeshift stage. There was a roar which the enemy must have heard up in the hills. She was a vision of an angel, to my tired eyes anyway. Her blonde hair may have been flattened by the sweat and the humidity, but her face and long legs were still a few shades closer to white than our burnt hides. She was wearing khaki in an imitation of our uniform but who cared what she wore. When she opened her mouth and let her voice take flight, well, it silenced the lot of us.

Yes, the songs were poignant and nostalgic, and we probably all suffered homesickness, but don't we always. She soon had the lot of us joining in the choruses and we sounded like we were all together for once. I thought of home. Were Mum and Dad still hanging on through the blitz? How was Dick doing in Africa? Was Betty still waiting for me or had she fallen for one of these GIs that everyone said were over there now.

I slept well that night. Perhaps a good sing is good for you. There were still the dreams, of course, well, nightmares, but I dreamt of this pale angel with the soaring voice who had come to encourage us towards the end. It was the end for some of course. Nobby bought it on our next patrol. I'll miss him but I'll get to keep my pay.

The Others

The following stories cover a wide variety of genres, written at various times in the last fifteen or so years.

Cup of Tea – Introduction

In March 2020 we were suddenly cut off from our writing groups, in person anyway, by the start of the first COVID lockdown. We did carry on meeting by Zoom. This was one of my first responses, done to the theme of "cup of tea".

Cup of tea

The phone pinged. Kev put his can down and stretched across the sofa to dig it out from under a cushion. He swiped the green mark and shouted at the device.

"Hi Mick, What's up?'

"Whatsapp. No, I'm not on that, I'm just giving you a call, mate."

"What do you say? Can't hear a word. Wait. I'll pause the telly." Kev fumbled with the remote and managed to silence the TV that dominated the small room.

"That's better Kev. What were you watching? It didn't sound like the usual morning show."

"Nah, Mick. Got meself Disney Add. I'm watching one of them superhero films, Avengers of the Galaxy or sumfin."

"Not my cup of tea, Kev. I've just had an exercise video on."

"Yer not doin exercise are you, Mick?"

"Nah, not me mate. Just watching the girl demonstrating the moves. She's pretty er, supple."

"My missus wouldn't have me ogling some bird on the box."

"Isn't she at work, Kev?"

"Got laid off. All the offices where she cleans shut up shop. They're all working from home."

"What she doing with her time off?"

"Working from home. She's decided the house needs a spring-clean."

"That's awkward for you mate. You'll have to move your butt from that sofa."

"Yeah, well, she's out at the mo'. Went off to Tesco. Been gone for hours."

"You could have gone with her, Kev."

"No point. They're only letting one person per house in at a time and they ain't even got their caf open while you wait. Anyway, she's not letting me go shopping again."

"Why's that Kev."

"Monf ago, she sent me to get some bog roll. How was I to know she meant one pack of eighteen."

"What did you think she meant, Kev?"

"Eighteen packs. I had a heck of job getting them in the Fiesta. Mind you, she's changed her tune now. Every time she's been since, the bog roll shelves have been empty."

"Clairvoyant of you, Kev."

"Clare who? You know Mick I'm fed up wiv this lockdown."

"Why's that, mate. You only go out to go down the pub."

"That's it. Why did they go and shut down our boozer? Tell me that Mick."

"Er, haven't they closed them all, Kev?"

"Yeah, but Stan would never 'ave any of that Corona stuff in his bar."

"That's true, mate."

"I wouldn't drink Chinese piss. Just good old British beer for me, Fosters or Stella. Oh, I can hear the missus now. Ta-ra Mick."

A cry came from the kitchen.

"Kev! You still watching that effing TV? How about a cup of tea?"

"Yeah, thanks, luv. That'll be great. I'm dying for a cuppa."

Reunion – Introduction

This piece came out of another of our lockdown Zoom group meetings. The phrase chosen as our prompt was "you're frozen Linda". I couldn't resist the play on words.

Reunion

It was that time of year again, and this time it was my turn to be the host. The first thing to do was dig out the Bain Marie from the back of the cupboard, fill it with water and set it on the hotplate to heat up. I didn't need it but it had to be seen to be used. Next was food preparation. The menu was always the same for our reunions. It had been set in stone since our first, that year after we graduated, nearly fifty years ago now. I don't know why we kept it up, just a couple of weeks before Christmas when things were getting frantic, but we did. No one missed, ever, not even with children being born; not until this year.

With the meal progressing I turned to laying the table. Out came the Lazy Susan. I placed it in the centre of the dining table and in its eight slots put small bowls of crisps (salted and cheese & onion), peanuts (salted and dry roasted), twiglets, Bombay mix, Hula Hoops and nuts & raisins. All our agreed and accepted hors oeuvres. Perhaps our tastes had got more sophisticated since then but, traditions are important, aren't they.

It was nearly time, so I told Alexa to start playing Christmas Carols. It had been a cassette that first time we'd met up, then a CD. The doorbell rang promptly at seven. Susan was always the first to arrive accompanied by Diane. We hugged and kissed and made rude comments about each other but there wasn't quite the usual outpouring of joy. We were going to be one short this year. I started pouring the first drinks, Bloody Marys of course, with extra Worcestershire sauce for Susan. Marie arrived soon after, followed by Carol and we sat around the table spinning the Lazy Susan.

We'd moved onto prosecco by the time supper was ready. Not traditional but well, you can't go wrong with a bit of fizz can you. The Steak Diane was cooked to perfection everyone agreed. Then it was time for dessert.

"Have you made it?" Diane said, a frown clouding her usually cheerful face.

"Of course, I have," I replied, "We can't have a reunion dinner without it."

"But, Mary," Carol said with a pause, "I wasn't sure you would with her not being here."

"We've got to," I said a little more firmly than I intended. "She would have wanted us to."

Susan took my side, "Of course, she would."

"I suppose it is a way of remembering her." Marie added.

I went to the freezer and drew out the bowl I had prepared earlier. It was bit like Eton Mess except she hadn't been able to get strawberries at Christmas time back then and she didn't have any cream. It was a mixture of crumbled meringue, tinned mandarins and cheap vanilla ice cream. I put a serving into five bowls. A tear trickled down my cheek as I remembered all those times when there were six of us.

I handed the bowls around the table. We all paused, spoons in hand, before we took our first mouthful.

Susan nodded. "Mmm, yes Mary, your Frozen Linda is wonderful, if not quite up to Linda's own standard."

We all laughed, more from relief at mentioning Linda's name than the annual reference to the dish named after our friend. She had always felt a little left out not having something bearing her name. The sweet she had cobbled together one evening late in the autumn term of our final year had been named in her honour and had cemented our friendships. Now she was the first one to leave; a brief vicious cancer had seen to that.

Everyone helped with the clearing and washing up. As we emptied the last bottle with a final toast to Linda, I turned to Susan.

"It's your turn next. Don't forget to take the Bain Marie and Lazy Susan. I don't want them cluttering up my cupboards for another year."

Shoes – Introduction

This was another COVID lockdown story though there is no reference to the pandemic in it. It does however draw on reports about another type of atrocity that afflicts the world. The theme set by the group was "shoes", but it was one image that drove the story.

Shoes

There were dozens of pairs of slippers and sandals of traditional style and manufacture, a scattering of worn trainers, their logos a symbol of the modern world, and a few smart leather brogues, imported at great expense by those with the cash to show off. They were lined up on the steps at the entrance, awaiting the return of their owners. They would remain unclaimed. The air was filled with dust and smoke and the stench of burned flesh.

Trucks arrived disgorging soldiers in a motley variety of uniforms, their heavy boots thudding on the dry, hard earth. They struggled to form a cordon around the mosque but already there were hundreds of people, many barefoot, crawling over the heap of rubble. Wailing alarms announced the arrival of white vans with red markings. Medical orderlies with plastic bags over their light plimsolls dived from them and ran into the smouldering ruin. Ignoring the bodies and bits of bodies, they searched for the living to assist and the dying to comfort. The soldiers remained outside, wary, expecting a second explosion; one strike was often followed by another.

Gwen Parry tightened the laces of her steel toe-capped safety shoes, pulled up the zip of her flak jacket and placed her helmet with its large PRESS sticker on her head. Ignoring the last dregs of her thick, sweet coffee she picked up her camera and joined the crowd moving towards the site of the atrocity.

Gwen elbowed her way between the crying people and evaded the soldiers trying to hold them back. She stood before what used to be the grand entrance to the mosque. Despite the sirens, the shouted orders and the wail of the crowd behind her, the scene before her was quiet. The rescuers were silent, pausing frequently from moving the lumps of concrete to listen for the faint cries of the trapped. Few came.

She took a few wide-angle shots to record the general scene of destruction, but Gwen did not venture into the carnage. Her audience would not want to see blood, shit and gore. Then she noticed the shoes. By some fluke of physics, they had been untouched by the force of the explosion which caused the building to collapse. They still rested in their neat rows. The uniform patina of grey dust made them appear like some modern work of art, a monument to the dead. She moved along the rows videoing in close-up, picking out the various styles, the state of wear, the sizes that reflected the age and wealth of their male owners. She wondered if there was a similar image to symbolise the female victims.

There was a pair of trainers, gold canvas just visible through the dust. Gwen knew those shoes. They belonged to a youth, a talented basketball player. She'd interviewed him recently in a café when he had told her of his dream of escaping to the US to play professionally among his heroes. How many other owners of these shoes had she met during her weeks based in the town? The old men who played interminable rounds of their traditional gambling games at the street-side cafes; the wealthy owner of the block of flats in which she was billeted; the teenage boys kicking a deflated ball down the dusty streets. No young men, of course, they were all in the militia, no doubt vowing vengeance for this and previous attacks.

Gwen glanced down at the ground and saw her own footwear was as grey and dust covered as the men's shoes. The dust of the dead.

The Necessity of a Raincoat – Introduction

A bit of a change here – something a bit older and more substantial. The writing group provided the brief, first paragraph. Everything else followed from that. How, you might ask. I'm afraid I have no idea. Likewise, the ending.

The Necessity of a Raincoat

It was 3 a.m. I'd missed the last bus. I hadn't enough money for a taxi and it had started to rain. My raincoat was hanging in the hall cupboard at home.

My mother always said, "don't forget your raincoat, you never know when you might need it". She was right. It was one of the essential tools of my trade. Mine was not the stereotypical trench coat. Pale beige with concealed buttons, it had two diagonal outside pockets. It just reached my knees, a compromise between the possibility of wet trouser legs and being able to run, and it had a thin collar just wide enough to put up and stop raindrops dripping off the brim of my hat. I can't say I was that attached to it as I had a habit of going through raincoats rather rapidly. Keeping rain off was just one of its assets but it was not much use in the cupboard when I was stranded five miles away.

I hadn't intended leaving home without it of course but I didn't get much choice in the matter. It was nine o'clock; the theme tune to Softly, Softly, Taskforce had faded out and I was thinking of bed – you have to make up for the night work sometime. There was a sharp tap on my front door. I opened it and found myself lifted off my feet by two goons, 6 foot and 18 stone, each of them. They carried me kicking and squealing to a car, a big one, a Wolseley, I think. They

48

shoved me in the back seat and got in, one on each side of me. The driver drove us off with no hesitation.

"Hiya boys," I said trying to appear relaxed about being dragged out of my own home.

"Shurrup," Gus, on my left, said, or it may have been George. With identical crew-cuts and black suits, they were easy to get confused.

"Where are we going?" I tried again.

"Shurrup," said George, or it may have been Gus. For added emphasis he showed me his fist, complete with brass knuckle duster. I had a fair idea where we were headed, unless this was my last trip, in which case I was bound for a shallow hole in a remote field. I was somewhat relieved when we headed into town and not at all surprised when we drew up at the "Golden Chip", not a fish restaurant but the town's brand-new casino.

The two burly boys marched me down an alleyway, through a side entrance and pushed me into a dark space. The lock clunked and I groped around finding that I was in a small storeroom. I tried out my locksmithing skills, such as they are, but was defeated. In fact, it was rather a secure door for a simple store, but the smell suggested it was used for holding animate or previously animate stock rather than mere paper goods. I sat down on the concrete floor to wait, knowing that my kidnapper was intending me to stew for a few hours.

It was gone 2 a.m. by the luminous dial of my watch when the door was flung open and my two friends dragged me out, blinking, into the dim electric light. They escorted me up a couple flights of scruffy stairs to their boss' office and stood me in front of them facing his large oak desk.

"Hi, Boyd," I said cheerily, not adding the 'Big' that usually went with the occupant of the leather chair behind the desk. He tended to get a bit sensitive about his nickname. Five foot four inches in his built-up shoes, big in stature he certainly wasn't, but he was big in the business of fraud, extortion, and any other illegal activity you care to mention. Big Boyd was the biggest big man in town. He'd even bribed the council planning officers to turn the town's third best cinema into a casino. He wanted to bring 1970s Las Vegas to a part of middle England that hadn't yet discovered the 60s.

He glared at me from the tiny dark eyes under his thick bushy brows and Brylcreamed black hair.

"Henley, isn't it? Private dick," he sneered.

"Joe Henley," I nodded, almost adding 'at your service' but there was no way I wanted to be in his service.

"You've been snooping," he said.

I didn't answer.

"I don't like people nosing around my property, particularly good for nothing losers like you."

I was a bit offended by his assessment of my skills but still I said nothing.

"What's your story?" he went on, his neck beginning to turn pink as his level of frustration grew. I didn't speak while I tried to think of a suitable answer.

"Look, you may think you're tough," he went on, "but my lads can soon have you chatting away as if your life depended on it." He didn't add 'which it may'. Actually, I'm your original ten stone weakling, so being tough is not one of my attributes.

I felt hot breath on the back of my neck as Gus or George panted with anticipation of a bit of violent recreation.

"I'm on a case," I said at last.

"Aren't you the lucky one. I'm surprised anyone would choose you to pack a case let alone solve one," he laughed at his little joke and Gus and George chuckled.

"It's a missing girl," I went on ignoring his banter. I thought I might as well tell him as I was damn sure he knew the story anyway.

"So, why have you been snooping around my business?"

"She was last seen coming into this place."

"Hundreds of people come here every night. The Golden Chip is a popular recreational establishment."

"But most come out again. This girl apparently didn't."

"Oh, come now," Boyd smiled and shrugged, "Everyone leaves sometime. She probably went off with some new friends."

"Perhaps," I conceded. It was those new friends that I was concerned about.

"I'd certainly know if someone was hanging round when we closed up, so you've no reason to be concerned on that score." He gave me his widest smile, the one that reminded me of a crocodile just about to snap.

"None at all, as you say."

"Well, I'm glad that's settled. Gus and George will see you out with a little reminder of what we think about snoopers." He nodded to my companions and dropped his head to read some papers. I was lifted by strong hands under my armpits and carried out. We returned to the side entrance. I suppose I hoped to be just thrown out but Gus and George were keen to carry out Boyd's final order.

How do you brace yourself for a beating? I've never found an answer. Gus or George held me up and George or Gus hit me in the stomach, first with his right and then his left. Then they threw me out.

I lay winded for a few minutes before I summoned the energy to haul myself to my feet, then staggered to the main road. It was quiet. The lucky and not so lucky punters had all left. The last bus was long gone. I had no money for a taxi, and it was starting to rain.

It was gone five when I made it home, wet, exhausted and sick. My front door was still open and the lights were on but speculative thieves had not made use of the opportunity, which was one cause for celebration. I crawled up the stairs, pulled off my soaking clothes and fell on the bed.

The alarm clock woke me a couple of hours later. I flung it off the bedside table feeling like death but forced myself to sit up. My abdomen ached and I was cold, but a long, hot shower helped me feel something like human. I couldn't face food, but a hot, sweet cup of tea brightened up my morning and I felt ready to contemplate the case.

Why was Big Boyd so concerned to warn me off the Lucy Miller case? Lucy was a nineteen-year-old student who considered university an opportunity to party. To Mr and Mrs Miller, she was still, nevertheless, their little princess, as pure and spotless as a fairytale heroine. When Lucy didn't 'phone them for a day or two, they got worried. Of course, the police weren't interested – how many students ring their parents every other day? So, the Millers came to me, convinced that Lucy was missing. It didn't take me long to find out that she was. None of her student friends or lecturers had seen her for days but, as I told Boyd, I had traced her as far as the Golden Chip. She'd told a girlfriend that she was going there, but who she went with I had yet to discover.

Perhaps Boyd thought that his warning would be enough to deter me, in which case he knew me less well than I knew him, especially as I now knew that my investigations had set his alarm bells ringing. I dressed, took my raincoat out of the cupboard and got the Austin 1100 out of the garage.

I parked a few streets from the casino and wandered down the High Street with my raincoat over my arm. It was a fine, early spring morning. The overnight rain had cleaned the place up and given it a fresh odour. There were more people around than at 3 a.m., quite a lot in fact, in and out of the butchers, bakers, grocers and hardware stores. I went into a little cafe opposite the Golden Chip and sat in the window sipping a hot, sweet tea. Nobody went into or came out of the old cinema building and there was no sign of the big Wolseley or Boyd's own Roller. I decided this was probably as good a time as any to do some real snooping.

I crossed the road and looked carefully left and right. At the end of the alleyway beside the casino I noticed some rubbish bins. It's always worth looking at what people have thrown out and my luck was in. Among the potato peelings and empty whisky bottles was a black and white mini dress. It was creased and dirty but there no stains that were obviously blood which was heartening. It was Lucy's. How did I know? Well, the name tag obviously sewed on by her loving mother gave it away. If her dress hadn't left then there was a chance she hadn't either. I had to give the casino itself a good going over, notwithstanding Boyd's warnings.

I drew my pistol from the pocket and wrapped the raincoat around my hand. A raincoat makes a satisfactory silencer and conceals the weapon from casual inspection. Then I tried the side entrance. It wasn't as strong as the door to the storeroom where I was locked up and gave with a good shove of my shoulder. I slipped inside, pulled the door closed and listened. There were no sounds of movement. I was hoping that the nocturnal crooks were safely tucked up in bed. I moved along the narrow corridor trying all the doors. Most were unlocked and opened to reveal nothing of interest. I climbed the stairs and searched the upper floors. I was getting a bit nervous of the time I was taking when I climbed the final flight to the attic rooms. The first door opened to reveal piles of old film cases and rolled up posters; a treasure trove for movie buffs but not what I was after.

I got to the last low door cut to fit the roof line. I tried the handle. It was locked. I thought I heard a noise and placed my ear against the wood. There were sounds muffled by more than the thickness of the door. I stepped back and charged. The door jamb splintered and I fell through. Something sharp hit my forehead and I struggled to regain my balance. I lifted the pistol ready to fire. The small room, a cupboard really, was lit by a hurricane lamp that had hung from the roof just inside the door and having made contact with my brow was now on the floor, fuel spilling out, catching alight. I grabbed my raincoat in my spare hand and beat at the fire, smothering the blue flickers before they became roaring orange flames. Panting, but reassured that I had not set off an inferno, I looked around. It was dark without the lamp but what I could see was pretty significant. On the floor with ankles and wrists tied, dressed in just knickers and a bra was a young woman. A pair of tights, hers I presumed, was tied around her mouth. She was wriggling and mumbling. Her eyes stared at me, wide open and scared.

"It's OK, Lucy," I said, "I'm a friend. I've come to get you." I bent down, feeling in my jacket pocket for my Swiss army knife. It took quite a few moments to cut through the ropes around her wrists then I set to releasing her ankles while she tugged at the gag. At last after much effort she was freed and struggled unsteadily to her feet, shivering.

"Are you the police?" she asked, quite understandably.

"No, and we need to get out of here quick, before someone comes back for you. Put my coat on." I offered my raincoat, now a little singed and covered in soot. She put her arms in the sleeves and wrapped it around her torso. I grabbed her arm with my left hand and dragged her from her cupboard, leading with my pistol.

There wasn't opportunity for conversation as we went down the flights of stairs, pausing on each landing to listen for sounds of other occupants of the building. My heart was thudding in my chest as I anticipated Boyd, Gus and George or any of his other bully boys appearing, but we reached the ground floor without incident and exited through the shattered side door.

The alleyway, enclosed on both sides by tall buildings seemed to stretch to infinity but it was our only route back to the civilised world of the High Street. I kept Lucy behind me, trying to hide or shield her just in case one or more of Boyd's employees appeared. I could hear her miserable sniffles and stifled squeals as her bare feet stepped on the sharp gravel. I dragged her along as fast as I could, waving the pistol in front of me, my trigger finger tensed. I wasn't afraid to fire in order to make our escape and thoughts of innocent bystanders barely passed through my head. I suppose it took us ten seconds to get to the road, but it felt like ten years. We burst out into the hustle and bustle of a daytime shopping neighbourhood. I pocketed my pistol, drew Lucy to my side and hurried down the pavement, zigging and zagging around shoppers and tradesmen. No doubt people looked at us and wondered but we were passed them before it occurred to them to question us.

We reached my parked 1100 and I bundled Lucy into the passenger seat. I ran around to get into the driving position and had the key in the ignition, engine running and in gear in one smooth movement. I pulled into the traffic and glanced at my passenger. She had folded in on herself with my raincoat wrapped tightly around her.

"I want to hear your story," I said as calmly and kindly as I could manage, "but we must get you somewhere safe." The question was where that might be. My house was the first place Boyd would think of looking when he discovered his loss, and Lucy's digs would be the second. A police station would be the normal, respectable answer, but in this town,

Big Boyd's fiefdom, I wasn't certain of where the loyalties of the boys in blue lay. I'd rescued Lucy, at the expense of one raincoat but I wasn't certain I could keep her safe. This story had some life in it yet.

The room at the top of the stairs – Introduction

'The room in the roof' was the topic suggested at writing club. Why, I cannot recall. Nevertheless, it got me thinking about what that room could be and resulted in this short piece, which is part memoir, part fantasy.

The room at the top of the stairs

Every evening, usually after I had yawned, Mum would say, "Off you go, darling, up the wooden hill to Bedfordshire," and that is what I would do – climb the steep path to the magical kingdom that was my bedroom. I would get ready for bed, but just before my eyes closed in sleep, I would climb the other stairs, the steps that lead to my room in the roof.

Some nights the room was my observatory. I would look up into the dark sky, wave to the Man in the Moon and blow kisses to the stars. I'd cheer the shooting stars racing across the sky and call to the geese towing the coaches laden with clouds and lightning.

Other nights, the room was the at the top of the highest tower of my castle. I'd watch my guards patrolling the battlements, my archers, with arrows notched aiming out of their niches, my knights in the courtyard below cleaning their swords while their esquires tended to the horses, and outside, across the broad moat, the campfires and tents and banners of my army protecting my land.

There again, it may be my treehouse, high in the branches of the tallest tree in the jungle. I'd have conversations with the multi-coloured parrots that came to visit me, and I'd wave to the monkeys leaping from bough to bough. I would lean right out of the window and peer down through the leaves to the ground below where I could hear elephants trumpeting and lions roaring.

Maybe, it was the control room of my submarine and I'd squeeze my eyes and peer through the periscope at the fishing swimming by. There would be a school of dolphin playing around us, escorting us, while rays lazily beat their wings as they travelled to who knew where.

Perhaps, it was at the top of mountains, covered by snow and ice. I would watch flakes falling from grey skies and laugh as penguins skied down the slopes and polar bears threw snowballs that were so large that when they hit their target, they exploded into blizzards that obscured the view.

One night when I reached my room, I found it walled in glass at the very top of the tallest building in the world. Even though the Sun had still not set, the sky above was dark. I gazed down at fluffy clouds and aircraft leaving vapour trails. Tiny helicopters like honeybees came and went from landing platforms on levels far below. The ground on which the tower rested was so distant I could not see it, but I could see half the world laid all around me.

And often, my room was just a room in the roof filled with trunks and packing cases containing all sorts of treasures – clothes of silks and satins, toys that I had requested but never received, gold crowns and silver wands, and a huge cloak of violet velvet that I threw over my shoulders to keep me warm. There was a padded stool to kneel on and a small window which I could open and lean out to feel the winter's air. I'd stretch out my hand and feel a few snowflakes settle and melt. A blackbird would land on the windowsill and offer me a piece of cherry cake. A mouse would leap out of the gutter, his whiskers vibrating and hand me a lump of cheese. We'd share the morsels and talk about the days that had been and the days to come and slowly my eyes would close and I would drift off to the land of sleep.

Snowdrops for St Dwynwen – Introduction

Writing group topics are often decided by the calendar – festivals, seasons, etc. This one wasn't actually – the topic was snowdrops – but it happened to be on St Dwynwen's day so I put the two together.

Snowdrops for St Dwynwen

25th January, St Dwynwen's Day, the day Welsh lovers enjoy a cwtch.

It happened to be St Dwynwen's Day. I was walking through the churchyard and under one of the tall, bare trees I saw a patch of snowdrops. They took me by surprise, their whiteness stark against the barren earth and the gnarled brown trunk. I stood, tears in my eyes, unable, unwilling to return home. How could I leave such beauty to go back to him?

I crouched to look closely at one of the flowers. I lifted its small, vulnerable head and felt how much it resembled me.

"Beautiful aren't they. Resilient too. They cope with the winter weather so well."

I looked up to see Ceri, although we hadn't met before then. My tear-streaked cheeks must have been visible. We talked, or rather, I talked. Ceri was an easy person to pour out my woes to. Our conversation gave me encouragement. Before we parted Ceri knelt and picked a single bloom. Was it illegal back in those days? I don't know, but I accepted the flower with gratitude.

Our paths crossed a few times in the year that followed, and we made an arrangement to meet under the tree on the next St Dwynwen's day. It was one of those cold, crisp sunny days when the snowdrops seemed to glow. We hugged and talked and hugged again. Ceri didn't pick another flower but pointed to the mat of snowdrops spread across the lawn.

"Snowdrops stand for hope, for new beginnings," Ceri said. "Perhaps their meaning will be true for you this year."

Those words stayed with me throughout the difficult times but by the end of that year I had left him and started to think about a new life. We met again under the tree amongst the snowdrops, but this time Ceri and I kissed and dedicated ourselves to each other. We combined our homes and looked forward to our lives spent together.

The years passed and we didn't get to spend every St Dwynwen's Day in the churchyard. Sometimes there was a covering of snow which buried the snowdrops, though those occurrences became rarer as time passed. Sometimes a gale was blowing, tearing boughs from the old trees. Year after year, we observed the snowdrops spreading until the whole churchyard seemed to turn into a sheet of white in January, a shroud perhaps.

So here I am again, on St. Dwynwen's day, alone in the churchyard. The old tree is just a stump now. It was chopped down last year because it was becoming unsafe. There are not many snowdrops in bloom; their peak has come earlier and earlier as the years have passed. I've come, alone, for the memories now. My head droops like the snowdrops and tears blur my sight.

We buried Ceri last week, in a meadow with hills surrounding it. That was what she wanted, to be at one with her country. I placed a posy of snowdrops, cultivated ones of course, on her grave, a symbol of my remembrance and the purity of our love, a recognition that death has parted us. Yet now as I continue my life alone, I know that I had her love and that every year that the snowdrops bloom she will be here with me.

The one that got away – Introduction

St Valentine's Day was the theme set for this effort. I suppose all of us have had a bit of fun with sending anonymous (but well signposted) Valentine "surprises". I think I have included most of them here.

The one that got away

I was munching a piece of toast when the doorbell rang, enjoying a relaxed breakfast unlike the rush of a working day. I hurried to the door, wrapping my dressing gown around me. The postman was smiling broadly when I opened the door. He held out a handful of small packages, considerably more than my usual delivery, which was just as well as I'd have to make arrangements to have my post collected.

"Happy Valentine's," he said, "someone's popular."

Taking the pile into my arms I felt somewhat lost for words. How should a woman of mature years react to receiving missives expressing love, and other desires, from a variety of men to whom one feels nothing at all? Oh, yes, this post was not unexpected and in no way gratifying.

I carried the post back to the kitchen and laid each item out on the table. Then I sat and stared at them. Would they be the same as last year? Probably. I suppose I could have just scooped them all up and dumped them in recycling, but I decided to open them, if only to separate the paper and cardboard from the other materials contained within, ready for collection

The first I chose was a long cylinder. Inside was, as expected, a clear cellophane tube containing a single red rose. Despite the little vessel containing water clamped to the stem, the rose was already past its best. The petals were curling and the head drooped. I tore open the packaging and put the poor thing into a slim vase. It wouldn't have long to live which was just as well in the circumstances. There was a small card attached to the tube. It had the picture of a vast bunch of red roses on the front and inside a handwritten verse.

> *Roses are red,*
> *Lilies are white,*
> *Let's go to bed,*
> *Your place tonight?*

"Not a chance," I said out loud. The card and rose were from Derek. We had sat a few desks apart from each other for all the years I had worked in the office. I suppose you might say we were friends, but I would prefer, acquaintances. We chatted occasionally over a coffee, but that was the extent of it. Derek was a similar age to me, that is, won't see forty again and looking at retirement approaching on the horizon. He was single and, as far as I could tell, had no interests whatsoever. His conversation revolved around the TV programmes he had watched the night before. That was the sum of our relationship and yet once a year, or perhaps twice if you count the occasion at the office Christmas party, the only time we had one, when Derek was suddenly filled with romantic lust or something that persuaded him to spend a few quid on a mass produced flower that hadn't had better days to see anything of.

The next parcel was rectangular and as predictable as the rose. It was a box of milk chocolates. I don't like milk chocolate, never have, but it wasn't surprising that Rupert in accounts didn't know, because he never spoke. He was a tall thin man with greying hair flattened down by grease, either his own or some proprietary brand. Each day he passed through our office without saying a word, but occasionally our eyes would meet. I would greet him and he would nod and hurry on. That brief but repeated encounter seemed to be sufficient for him to consider me his valentine and one true love. The card covered in hearts and the printed rhyme stated that clearly but words of his own there were none.

The third and last parcel was soft and rustled as I picked it up and squeezed it, again, not that I was unaware of the contents. I tore the brown paper off to reveal a set of lingerie; a bra and knickers in red, lacy fabric although it had obviously been nowhere near the skilful if hardened fingers of lace makers. The pants wouldn't have covered the embarrassment of a hamster, or the bra held a couple of fried eggs. The label revealed that the garments were part of a value range of a certain supermarket. Whether they were intended to be worn or just intended as props to accompany the card, I don't know. It would require an imagination of Hollywood epic proportions to envisage my aging form squeezed into such underwear but actually, the fact that they were two sizes too small showed that my valentine had no imagination at all. He was Cecil, an overweight, overheated client who visited our office about once a month. Unfortunately, it fell to me to comply with his many requests and deal with his frequent complaints. I coped with the chore with all the professionalism I could muster but I must have been doing something to his satisfaction as he had selected me as the focus of his affections. How he'd ever be able to do anything with me or anyone else wearing just the supposedly sexy "skimpies" that he bought every year was beyond me. He'd have a heart attack if he ever tried anything as energetic as intercourse.

Just as I was sorting the gifts and cards for the bins, I heard something else drop through the letter box. I went to pick up the envelope from the mat. It was very large and had only just fitted through the slot. There was no stamp, revealing that it had avoided passing through the hands of the Royal Mail. There was no need for their assistance as it had come from next door, delivered by my neighbour, Henry, a man of the most amazing scruffiness, with hair emerging from ears and nostrils as well as sticking out at all angles from his head and face. Ever since he had moved in three years ago, he had looked on me as the solution to the problem of his bachelorhood. I had taken to hiding inside whenever he went out into his garden but luckily that was not very frequent as his small patch was turning into a wilderness. Not that that had entirely pleased me as it reduced the price of my house. I had also feigned absence on the occasions when he came knocking.

I opened the envelope and extracted the huge card. The picture was very simple – two horribly cute teddies in an embrace. Inside, above, below and across the mandatory saccharine verse, was scrawled, in letters as rough as if they'd been carved into a tree, the words 'to the woman of my dreams. XXX'. The thought of being the subject of Henry's dreams or fantasies made me feel sick and I tore the card up into tiny pieces and dropped them in the waste bin.

I hurried upstairs to get away from the debris left by my four valentines' entreaties. My case was beside the bed, packed and ready. All I had to do was get dressed and await the taxi. Soon I would be leaving the February cold behind and jetting off to sun, sea and sand – and Valentino, the sexy Spanish waiter who awaited me.

Look to the future – Introduction

Usually at Christmastime I write a festive piece, whatever theme is set by the group. Many count as SF or fantasy. Often, they're irreverent, often, they're humorous. This one's a bit different.

Look to the future

"So here it is, Merry Christmas…"

That damn Slade song, Billie thought. How long has Noddy Holder been screeching it? Every year for fifty years, over and over, resolutely jolly. She shuffled along the queue in the aisle as the music resounded over shoppers' heads.

"Everybody's having fun…"

Everybody? Like heck. Billie looked in her trolley. A few old potatoes, reduced price carrots, a couple of tins of "value" baked beans, a loaf of bread almost out of code, and her one extravagance – a turkey dinner ready meal for one. That would be her Christmas if the meter had enough left on it to run the microwave. She reached the single checkout which had a human operator and dug in her bag to find her remaining change to pay the bill.

Billie trudged towards the exit, her bag for life hooked over her arm. It wasn't very heavy.

"Look to the future now…"

There was a bright light ahead. It wasn't sunlight shining in from the carpark outside. It was a dull day. No, it came from all around her, washing out the supermarket shelves, the towering displays, the ceiling and walls. There were people in the light like shadows. No, not shadows, wraiths, beckoning her. She stumbled forward.

"Come and join us," they said, "this is your future now."

She recognised the figures. There was Mam, a young mother, looking like she did when Billie had been a child; Dad, with hair, standing upright, not bent like he was in old age; brother Dick, a teenager, grinning, urging her on. There were others – aunts, uncles, cousins, neighbours, school friends, colleagues. All smiling, drawing her into the light.

"Hey, that old dear's fallen over."

"She's demolished that pile of crackers. Is she drunk?"

"She looks as though she's fitting. Perhaps it's a stroke."

"Oh, god, she's pissed herself."

"Has anyone called an ambulance?"

"That'll take for ever."

"Excuse me, let me through. I'm the store first-aider."

They weren't the Mam and Dad and Dick she recalled. Dad took a belt to her four days out of five; Mam locked her in the coal shed without supper; Dick punched and kicked and pinched her when no-one else was looking; and the others – miserable sods, bullies, abusers, bigots. Yet here they were pulling her towards them.

"Come on William."

"Join us, Bill."

"What are you waiting for Whiting?"

Billie muttered. "No, I'm not that boy. I'm Billie, like Billie Whitelaw." Her idol, the beautiful actress with a name almost the same as hers.

"She's breathing funny."

"Help me loosen her clothes, I need to get air into her."

"Good god, it's a bloke."

"She's going."

"But he's wearing a dress."

The light shone all around her. She was part of the crowd, pressed in on all sides, carried along. Everyone was still smiling.

"Everything will be fine now, William."

"We're heading into the future, Bill."

"I'm Billie, not William or Bill. Billie."

"Yes, but that doesn't matter now. The future will be wonderful."

"...It's only just begun."

Sisters - Introduction

This story has a similar theme to the previous one although it is in fact older. It was written to satisfy the topics set by the two writing groups that I attend – "road not taken" and "jealousy". It is a story that is close to me although none of it at all is autobiographical.

Sisters

My sister has beautiful long, fair hair with just a hint of curl. It feels so silky and shines in light. I wanted hair like it. More than that I wanted her blue eyes, whipped cream skin and infectious giggle. I wanted to be my sister.

With Dad at work all the time and Mum busy around the house and so on, I was left in the care of my sister when I was little. Four years older than me, she viewed me as her plaything, her living doll. She dressed me in her cast-off princess dresses, painted my nails, put lipstick on my lips and blusher on my cheeks. She combed my mousy brown hair and wheeled me around in the pushchair.

More and more as we grew older, I wanted to be like her, to be her. One day when she was dozing, I snipped off some of her curls. Why? Who knows? Perhaps I intended sticking them on my head or maybe I just wanted a bit of her to keep. I followed her everywhere. When she began dance lessons, so did I.

She came out of her bedroom to find me standing on the landing. I was wearing the pink satin dress, the last one I had. She'd moved on from princesses so there were no more hand-me-downs, and this was the only one that still fitted. I had brushed my hair and put ribbons in it. I'd put on bright pink lipstick that matched the dress.

"What are you doing?" she said.

"I wanted to tell you something," I replied.

"What? I haven't got time now. I'm meeting Milly and Saffron."

"No. Please. I just wanted to say. . ."

"Say what?"

"I want to be a girl." I paused. That hadn't come out as I intended. "I mean, I am a girl. I know I'm a girl."

"Don't be silly. You're a boy. You've got a willy." She pushed me out of her way and hurried to the stairs. She paused and looked back at me. "Oh, god. It's my fault. All those years of dressing you and making you up. I've turned you into a freaking tranny."

She scampered down the stairs. A moment later the front door slammed. I went back to my room, threw myself on the bed and cried.

It was after bedtime when I heard footsteps on the stairs. They were too light for Mum or Dad. Anyway, they'd be asleep on the sofa supposedly watching TV. My door opened and I recognised the silhouette. It was my sister.

"Are you awake?" she whispered. I turned over to show her I was. "What you said earlier; did you mean it?"

I pushed myself up in the bed eager to try again.

"I want you and Mum and Dad and everyone to know I'm a girl, to let me be a girl when I start high school."

She shook her head, "I gave you these stupid ideas, didn't I? All that dressing up." Her face crinkled.

"No, no. I loved all that stuff. I enjoyed the dressing up, the make-up. Do you think I'd have let you do it if I didn't want it?"

She stood up, backed away. "You were so little back then. I wasn't thinking. We're older now. You do your own thing, dancing and stuff."

I grabbed her hand and dragged her back to me. "I started dancing because you did."

"But you're so much better than me. You could do it for a job."

I shrugged. "Perhaps. I'll be a girl dancer."

"But you're a boy!"

I shook my head. "I can have my willy taken away. Doctors can do that. Then I'll be a girl like you. I'll get boobs." Hers had started to appear during the last year and I often stared at them enviously.

"You really think you want to go through all that. The bullies will have a field day if you turn up at school in a skirt. Then there's the drugs and the surgery. I've seen it on YouTube. It's awful."

"It's what I want. Will you help me get Mum and Dad sorted?"

She looked at me with large sad eyes and didn't say anything for a while.

"OK, but don't say anything yet. Let me think about it."

Next day a letter arrived saying I'd won a scholarship at Performing Arts school. After that there wasn't time to think about anything except getting prepared for going away. At school I met musicians, actors and dancers, boys as well as girls. I loved it. The year passed in a blur of hard work and fantastic experiences. Back home for the summer holiday I noticed that I was now taller than my sister. Only her bust had grown in the last year. I bet that was one of the attractions for the boyfriend who she spent all her time with while waiting for her exam results.

I continued to get taller. My shoulders widened, hairs grew in various places, my voice dropped, and I discovered what a willy can do. My hair stayed long and I wore makeup, not only on stage. I pulled on a dress from time to time too. I took shit from some screwed-up people, but most couldn't give a hoot. I didn't know if I was a boy or a girl and didn't care. I was me. But I still wish I had my sister's hair.

The Addict – Introduction

The theme set for the week was "the addict" but I didn't want to write about a typical addiction to illegal substances as I'd have to do some research on the symptoms. My subject's addiction was something much more familiar.

The Addict

The new day had not dawned when Greg tumbled out of bed and limped to the bathroom. Sleep had refused to come. His heart was beating rapidly in his chest. His skin felt warm and sweaty and his eyes just wouldn't focus. He stood under the shower for a few minutes, repeatedly soaping himself, forgetting which "bits" he'd done. At last, he tired of the patter of water on his head, stepped out and grabbed the threadbare towel from the hook. He didn't feel cleaner, didn't feel more awake, just damp.

He dressed in an old t-shirt and grubby jeans and went to his small kitchen. He didn't need to look in the fridge and cupboards, but he opened doors, nevertheless. There was no food. Of course, there wasn't. He hadn't been shopping for food for days. There were a few grains of coffee left in the jar. He held the kettle shakily under the tap, then spilt water down his trousers as he moved it to the socket.

Greg took his mug of weak coffee into the living room, squeezing between the piles of books to reach his one easy chair. He sat down but couldn't feel comfortable so stood up again and moved around the room, lifting books here and there, glancing at the titles, opening to a random page, reading a few lines, then putting the book back down.

He couldn't go on like this. He needed a fix. Greg thrust his hands in his pockets. They were empty. He returned to the bedroom and searched the pockets of his old corduroy jacket. Joy! A few coins. He counted them; more than three pounds.

Anticipation filled him with eagerness to get out. He pulled on the jacket and hurried from the flat. He all but leapt down the stairs, almost stumbling on the bottom step and strode out, onto the street.

The day had started now. People were on their way to work. The pavement became more occupied as he neared the town centre. He bustled through the crowd, occasionally jostling someone walking more slowly or coming towards him. A few people reacted calling insults or elbowing him back, but he didn't respond, staggering on towards his goal.

He passed the shops in the high street, though most of them were open now. The odour of fresh bread from the bakers did not attract him even though his belly felt empty. He turned into a side street and stopped at a small shopfront. The door was closed. He pushed on the handle. It didn't move. He rattled the door in its frame then tapped firmly on the glass.

"Alright, don't break the door down," a muffled voice called from deep inside the shop. Greg responded by knocking again. "OK, I'm coming," the voice said, growing louder as the speaker approached. A hunched figure appeared behind the grubby window in the door. There was some fiddling with the lock and then the door swung open.

"Oh, it's you," the straggly-haired shopkeeper muttered, shuffling backwards. Greg pushed through the door and stopped.

The familiar, delicious odour filled his nostrils. It was almost enough to still the pangs of desire. Almost. Greg moved into the interior of the shop until he was surrounded by the ceiling high shelves and heaps of stock. All was covered by that particular kind of dust that collected in second-hand and antiquarian bookshops, the spores of the

73

fungus that grew within the pores of the old paper and gave off that delicious perfume.

After a few moments, the pleasure of absorbing the atmosphere of the dimly lit emporium faded and Greg re-experienced the need to search.

"Got something you're looking for?" the aged bookseller asked.

"Er, nothing in particular," Greg replied his eyes scanning the stacks.

"I've got a first edition Graham Greene, just come in," the old man said shuffling to the battered captain's chair beside the ancient cash desk. He had to squeeze between tottering piles of books to do so.

Greg felt a pang of lust. "A Greene, you say. Which one?"

"Er, it's here somewhere." He lifted books from a pile until he came to the one he was seeking. "Here it is, The End of the Affair, hardback."

Greg's heartbeat faster, his palms became sweaty. He felt desire, he wanted that book. He imagined it on his shelves alongside the other Greenes, not that he could recall precisely where that shelf was.

"Let me see."

The old man passed the book to Greg. He saw immediately that the dust jacket was torn. He opened the cover, noting their stiffness. He turned the yellowing pages, breathing in those fumes that stoked his need. "How much?"

"Ninety-five."

"Pounds?"

"You didn't think pence, did you? It's a first edition."

"Yes, of course. Um, you couldn't give me…"

"Credit? Don't ask. Cash, that's all I take. You know that. Do you want it?"

Greg caressed the Greene. Of course, he wanted it but all he had were the few coins in his pocket. He handed the book back. "No, not today. Perhaps some other time."

"I'm not holding it for you." The bookseller put the book back on the pile.

"No, no, I understand. I'll just take a look at the paperbacks."

"Well, you know where they are. Don't muddle them up."

Greg snorted as he moved towards the back of the shop, deep into the gloom. Don't muddle them up. As if the old man kept things in order. Greg wondered if he'd ever heard of the Dewey system. He leaned close to the shelves trying to read the titles on the creased spines of the old paperbacks in the light of a single dim yellow bulb. His finger shook as he levered out a slim copy of The Far Country by Nevil Shute. Beads of sweat formed on his brow as he turned the beige pages. This was one of Shute's novels that he didn't possess. It was a well-thumbed copy but there were no obvious missing pages, no tears. He turned back to inside the front cover. There was some pencil scribbling on the facing page and a figure, £4. Yes, he had that much, he was sure. He pulled the coins from his pocket, three pound coins and a couple of fifty p's. He closed the book and clutched it to his chest.

Greg headed back to the entrance. He considered walking straight out, was reaching for the door handle.

"You found something then," the bookseller rumbled.

Greg stopped and turned, filled with guilt for even considering the theft.

"Er, yes. Four pounds. Here it is." He held out his palm holding the cash.

The old man thrust out his hand. "Let me see."

Greg gave him the book. The shopkeeper glanced inside the cover. "Yes, four pounds." He took the coins and deposited them in his cash machine with a clanging of bells and gears. Greg grabbed the book and dashed from the shop.

He made his way home feeling elated. The town seemed brighter, people on the streets more cheerful. He was content. Back in his flat, he held his prize to his nose, inhaling the familiar smell, then went from bookcase to bookcase looking for the other Shute novels he possessed. There they were, a half dozen similar old, slim paperbacks with small print and cheap rough paper. He slid the new acquisition onto the shelf beside the others. He took a step back, proud of his collection. There was a small itch at the back of his head. Maybe he could complete his set of Shute's novels. Just a few more, perhaps one or two at a time. He'd only need a few quid. His fingers twitched.

Torch – Introduction

This piece was written early in 2012 and the theme was, of course, the London Olympics. It seems strange now how exciting it was in the lead up to the Olympics themselves. Even the torch procession attracted crowds as this story suggests. Looking back, it seems like an unbelievable time of hope and anticipation, pride and satisfaction.

Torch

"Now, have we got everything," Mother asked looking over the heap of baskets, folding chairs, blankets and rainwear that filled the hallway of their small house.

"Aw, Mum, it's only a silly torch," Harry moaned, "Why can't I stay home and play."

"You know you're too young to leave on your own and anyway it's not silly. It's a once in a lifetime experience – longer, because I don't suppose the Olympics will ever be here again."

"Yes, but it will be gone in a flash. Why do we need all this stuff, we're not going away for a month."

"To get a good position to watch the torch relay, we have to get there early," Mother insisted, "We'll need something to eat and somewhere to sit. Granddad won't be able to stand for long, and it looks like rain, so we need our wet weather gear."

Harry's eyes glazed over and he slouched against the wall of the hallway. Mother looked up at Granddad coming slowly down the stairs, leaning heavily on the banister.

"Now Dad, have you got everything you need?"

Granddad reached the bottom and, breathing heavily, touched all the pockets of his old tweed jacket. He pulled out his pipe, a packet of tobacco, a sharp pointy thing, a pipe cleaner and a box of matches.

"Yep," he said, "all here."

Then he felt his head. His frayed cap was perched there, protecting his bald head from sun, rain or frost, whichever season it happened to be.

"All set," he said, "Hey, Harry, isn't this exciting. I never thought the Olympic Games would come here again."

Mother shook her head and sighed. "Harry, pick up a few things and take them to the car; and look after your sister,"

"Do I have to?"

"Yes, Harry you do. Try and be responsible for once."

Harry picked up a bag and opened the front door. Mother started to fill her arms with the remaining equipment and supplies.

They were the first at the corner. Mother had been planning for months and had chosen the position with care. The bearer of the torch would be turning the bend and so they would have a good opportunity to see him (or her) and the torch. It was a nice grassy verge with a tall hedge close behind so not too many people would crowd around them, and they'd been able to park the car just down the road, off the route. Chairs were unfolded, cushions arranged, blankets wrapped around Granddad and the food rations were broken into.

"I remember the 1948 torch," mused Granddad puffing on his pipe, "Now that was a fine piece of engineering."

"What's special about a silly torch?" Harry said, "Why not use an electric light. LEDs would be great, or a laser. Or, I know - a light sabre."

"There's no such thing as light sabres," little sister Mo said.

"What do you know about it? You're too young," Harry said. Mo began to cry and Harry got a telling off from Mother.

"You know, lad," Granddad said thoughtfully, "It's a difficult problem to make a torch that will keep burning for the whole time it's being carried along by a runner. A good gust of wind could blow it out."

Gradually more people joined them on the roadside, not that most people had come for an extended stay. By noon there were people on both sides of the road and they were starting to peer at watches.

"Won't be long now," Mother said eagerly.

"I feel sick," Mo moaned.

"You shouldn't have eaten all your sweets at once," Harry said.

"Just sit still," Mother said hopefully, "the torch will be along in a minute or two."

"I think it's going to rain," Granddad observed.

Harry looked up into the sky; the clouds had certainly grown larger and darker. Now they covered the sun. The air had become cold and they were surrounded by gloom. Harry held out the palm of his hand and was not surprised when a large drop of water landed on it.

"Oh, dear, we'd better get our macs on," Mother cried, rummaging in bags and pulling out waterproofs. The four of them and other members of the crowd stretched arms and contorted themselves, pulling on rainwear, while others clustered together hunching their shoulders and trying to make themselves smaller to avoid the rain drops.

The rain was falling hard now, a typical spring shower. In no time at all everywhere and everything was soaked by the downpour. The drops splashed as they hit the tarmac of the road. The dried-on bits of soil, dropped by the tractors, soon turned into soft, dark dollops of greasy mud. As quickly as it started, the rain eased to a steady drizzle. There was a commotion up the road.

"They're coming," Mo shouted, jumping up and down, her aching tummy forgotten.

"Can't see anything through this mizzle," Granddad complained.

"No, there he is," Harry said. Appearing out of the wet haze was a posse of people and at the front, an athlete carrying the flaming torch. He had greying hair and a bit of a paunch, but Harry thought he'd seen his picture in the local paper.

Mother waved the Union Jack flag she'd brought specially.

The cheering and gesticulations of the crowd moved along the road like a Mexican wave just in front of the runner. He kept to the middle of the road, keeping up a steady pace with the golden torch lifted high. Mother was cheering loudly now and Granddad had struggled to his feet. Even Harry felt excited. This was the flame that would light the Olympic beacon in a few weeks' time. Seeing it for real seemed to prove to Harry that the Olympic Games really were going to happen.

The torch bearer and his followers came to the bend and turned and that is when it happened. To Harry it seemed like a slow-motion replay. One moment the runner was running, the next his feet slid out from under him and he was falling. His feet went different ways, he flung out his hands to protect himself when he hit the road and the torch flew through the air. It hit the ground and rolled along until it stopped in the grass at Harry's feet. He bent down to pick it up.

"No, you can't touch it," Mother said, "only the bearers can touch it." Harry picked it up anyway.

"It's gone out," he said looking into the top of the torch. There were definitely no flames.

"Gone out!" Mother cried, "It's not allowed to go out."

"I said it was a problem keeping them lit," Granddad said.

The runner was being helped to his feet by his minders. He was grumbling loudly about mud on the road and asking where the torch had gone. The rain had stopped and the sun was shining again.

"Quick. Do something," Mother urged waving her hands and hopping from one leg to another.

"What?" Harry asked staring at the torch in his hand. People were starting to look at them and pointing.

"Don't let them see it's gone out," Mother said.

"Here, lad," Granddad reached into his pocket and pulled out his box of matches. He picked out a match and with the dexterity of many years of practice he had it lit in moments. He shielded it with his hand and held the flame close to the top of the torch. The fuel ignited and an almost invisible cloud of blue flame rose from the torch. Harry felt the heat on his face.

"Whoa, nearly lost your eyebrows there, lad," Granddad said. Harry turned to face the road grasping the burning torch with both hands.

"I'll take that," the runner said. He didn't look at Harry or Granddad but grasped the torch with his right hand, pulled it from Harry's grip and turned away. The runner lifted the torch up and returned to his position in the middle of the road. The crowd cheered. Moments later the torch bearer was lost in his pack of followers moving down the road. The people that had been passed by the torch began to drift away. Mother started packing the bags. Harry stood in the road watching the torch party disappearing in the distance, the cheering crowd oblivious to the drama that had occurred at the corner.

"Do you think anyone noticed that the flame had gone out?" Harry said.

"Oh, I hope not," Mother replied.

"What would have happened if we hadn't lit it?" Harry asked.

"The Olympics couldn't happen without a fire," Mo said.

"It's not quite that serious," Mother said, "But it would have been embarrassing if the flame had gone out."

"And it would have been on the TV and in the newspapers," Granddad added.

"Do you mean, I could have been famous if we hadn't lit it," Harry said with a disappointed tone to his voice.

"Famous as the boy who held the torch that went out," Granddad said, "Would you really want that?"

"I don't suppose so," Harry sulked.

"It was our responsibility to keep the Olympic flame alive," Mother said lifting her head up proudly.

"Well, I guess we did our bit," Granddad said, "The Olympics can go on now."

All Plaided and Plumed – Introduction

For some reason that I no longer recall, the topic for this week's writing was "tartan". I did a brief bit of research to find out when Scotland adopted tartan as a national symbol and came across the incident related here. I also decided to write totally in dialogue. Perhaps all nations have "traditions" based on imagination and whimsy rather than history. Wales has its druids while Scotland has its tartan kilts.

All Plaided and Plumed

"Good day, Lady Anstell. Oh, dear you seem to be a little damp."

"I regret I am, Lady Macgregor. The weather is not at all summer-like."

"Ah, I'm afraid it is for Scotland. You are a visitor and will find that Edinburgh is often wet during August. My maidservant will take your coat and hat. Please sit and take tea."

"It is very kind of you, Lady Macgregor, to welcome me. I am so eager to hear about your presentation to the King, the Saturday before last."

"Of course. It was a most joyous occasion at Holyrood, although not without a certain amount of tedium as we awaited our turn."

"The King, I believe, was something of a, er, picture?"

"I think Lady Anstell, you are understating the comments that have been circulating."

"The King was in Highland dress?"

"Well, it depends on what you understand by Highland dress. My great-grandfather wore the full belted plaid when he strode across the mountains. I believe it was Sir Walter's interpretation of the costume that the King wore."

"I had forgotten you have highlander blood, Lady Macgregor."

"It was not something that was admitted to for years after the forty-five, but sentiments have changed in recent times."

"Indeed, they have. But, King George, Lady Macgregor, tell me about him."

"Yes, my dear, I shall. He is, um, a big man."

"Big? I have heard others use less polite words to describe his figure."

"Well, you are probably right, Lady Anstell. He certainly has flesh to spare."

"And he was wearing a short kilt in tartan."

"Yes, it was the bright red, Royal Stuart, a striking design, though one whose purpose is to conceal the loss of blood in battle, not draw attention to oneself. The problem was that the King's kilt was, indeed, short."

"Exposing his knees, I hear, Lady Macgregor?"

"And a considerable area of thigh, Lady Anstell, though he was wearing pantaloons of a flesh pink to cover his skin."

"That does sound quite a striking sight."

"It was, particularly as he was festooned with gold chains, a sword, dirk and pistols with plumes of feathers in his hat."

"Oh, Lady Macgregor, I am filled with amazement. Yet, I hear that was the only time on his visit that he wore the outfit."

"I can't imagine that he felt particularly comfortable, Lady Anstell. Nevertheless, Sir Walter, got his way."

"To what do you refer, Lady Macgregor."

"Well, all the clan chiefs and their followers turned up at the balls wearing the same short kilts in a variety of tartans.

It was said that the pride of the clans has been re-invigorated and that they will wear this fancy dress again."

"That will be a sight to behold, all those men displaying their knees beneath colourful tartan. It is enough to make one swoon, Lady Macgregor."

"One will have to get used to it I am afraid, Lady Anstell. I don't think it will be long before us ladies are also clothed in tartan."

"Oh dear. Are we all to be Highlanders now?"

"Indeed we are, Lady Anstell. Scotland has discovered a history it never knew it had. One of Sir Walter's own invention."

Silver Spoon – Introduction

This is a curious piece. I am not sure what I was aiming for other than telling a story that fitted the topic of the week. The theme was the phrase "licking the spoon of life" and that combined with "being born with a silver spoon in one's mouth" rather set the tone.

Silver Spoon

The birth of the Honourable William Arthur Henry George Featherstonehaugh du Boit was greeted with joy by the great families with daughters across the land and reported in the broadsheets. The Earl took one cursory look at his first born, pronounced him fit to be the heir and passed him into the hands of the wet nurse. William spent his infant years in the care of nursery nurses working shifts, then in the not so tender hands of a succession of governesses. At the age of seven the Earl's number two carriage took him to boarding school. After an initial period of beatings and abuse he quickly learned how to bully, cheat and bribe his way to the top of the class. He completed school as Head Boy, Captain of Cricket and with a host of prizes, never having excelled in anything, performed on the pitch or revealed leadership qualities. Of course, he gained a place at Oxford where he majored in hunting, shooting and fishing with most of his effort spent smoking, drinking, gambling, whoring, beating servants and in general disorderly behaviour.

At the age of twenty-one he graduated and came into his majority. His father promptly died and he returned to the ancestral estates to take over the earldom. At his father's funeral he did not shed a tear as he knew nothing of the man, nor did he comfort his weeping mother as she had never held him in his life. He packed her off to one of their smaller estates on the far side of the country. He resumed his life of debauchery, bedding many eligible spinsters until he found one who he felt he could bear to look at for more than one day and who had inherited almost as much as himself. Their union was the wedding of the century but by the time his wife was safely in child he was bored. He returned to his coterie of friends and hangers-on who drank his wine, smoked his cigars, slapped the maids' bottoms and lounged on his gilded chairs.

They joked. "The Earl was born with a silver spoon in his mouth."

"Silver? More like a golden one."

"Definitely not gilt or he would have licked off the gold by now."

One day, he wandered alone in the gardens followed by a single servant encumbered with hamper, folding chair, shot gun and other items he might have need of. A bird fluttered above his head. He looked up. A dollop of dropping splattered on his forehead. He raged and demanded the servant wipe it off, then marched into his steward's office.

"I want no birds on my estates," he demanded.

"No birds?" the steward muttered. He trembled as he knew no employee was safe in the face of the earl's anger.

"No, not one. I am not giving another the opportunity to shit on me. See to it."

The armoury was opened up and the Earl, his friends, the servants, and the tenant farmers embarked on an avian killing spree. The estate was filled with the sound of gunfire. The birds rose into the air. Many were killed but most flew away.

The day after, the estate was quiet. Not a single bird fluttered in the branches of the trees, there was no twittering or cries in the bushes. Taking a walk through the silent woods the Earl paused. Surely, he could hear something, a faint chirruping. He located the source of the sound beneath a shrub. There he found a tiny fledgling sparrow. He picked it up. The little bird nestled in his hand its beak open, demanding food. He carried it back to the house and entered the kitchen. He spoke to the cook.

"This chick needs to eat. Feed it."

The cook looked at the bird with distaste. "Why, Sir? Yesterday you demanded that all birds be killed."

"That was yesterday. This is today." He placed the bird on a table. "Today I desire you to ensure this bird lives."

The cook took a silver sugar spoon, the smallest she could find, and fed the little bird with a little porridge. The Earl watched as the bird swallowed and appealed for more.

"Greedy, little thing, isn't it?" he commented.

"Is it greed to want a full stomach?" The cook said, immediately regretting her boldness.

The Earl appeared not to notice her insubordination but seemed to be lost in thought. "Is that all that is needed to satisfy such a creature?" he mused, "Yet what satisfies me? I find no lasting happiness in any pleasure. I have licked the silver spoon I was born with all my life and not reached that happy state."

He trudged from the kitchen, head bowed and full of sadness.

White Goods – Introduction

The prompt for this piece was "white goods" but it wasn't fridges and washing machines that came into my mind.

White Goods

The boat is back. Its masts rise from the sea to the sky, bearing the huge white sails. Its body is bigger than the whales that swim in the deep water. Now, the white men are coming to shore in their smaller boats. They do not look white in the clothes that cling tight to their bodies. Their faces are only slightly paler than my own, but I have seen their skin beneath the cloth. I have seen them when they come to poke my sister. Their bare buttocks and skinny thighs are as white as salt.

The captain steps ashore in his blue coat and hat. Our King greets him. The King shows he is delighted to welcome the white men again though I wonder whether his pleasure is as great as it once was. The men from the ship will be tired and hungry. They will expect to be fed and looked after by our women, my sister amongst them. The King will give them a pig to roast and fruit we have harvested. Our women will bear pale-skinned children, those that do not die of the diseases the white men bring upon us.

The King is pleased because the captain of the white men's boat brings white goods. Beads of all shapes and sizes and colours that we make into necklaces and bracelets and skirts to adorn our bodies and curtains to hang in our homes. They bring us firewater. The men drink it. It makes them loud and bold and boastful, then they argue and fight. Then they fall in a stupor and awake to start all over again. The King's biggest prize is the fire tubes. With them are wooden barrels of black powder and crates of the heavy, grey metal beads. The fire tubes give the King a way to wage war on our neighbours. Letting off the fire tubes fells warriors before they can get close to fight with clubs and blades. The King overcomes his enemies with ease and takes many prisoners.

What do we want with prisoners? Nothing, but the men, women and children, all that fall into our hands, are ours to give to the Captain. They become white goods. They are packed on the boat, and they leave us to travel across the western sea. They are never seen again.

Again and again, the boat returns, each time demanding more people to carry off. First it was dozens, then hundreds, now thousands and thousands have been sent across the water. The King sends his warriors with the fire tubes far inland to find new tribes that have not been raided. We neglect our crops, living off that which we steal from our neighbours. Still, the Captain demands more prisoners in exchange for their white goods. We fear that if the King fails to take enough captives, the white men will take us instead. We will have to go across the sea, who knows where and for what purpose. We will be the property of the white men. We will become white goods.

Traffic – Introduction

I had a bit of fun with this one, calling on some memories of holiday road trips. The topic was "traffic" but we decided to write a three way conversation without description. The task was to make each voice distinctive. Did I succeed?

Traffic

"Are we nearly there yet, Mummy?"

"No, darling, as you can see, we are not moving and haven't done since you asked five minutes ago."

"Why aren't we going anywhere, Mummy?"

"Well, Daddy can answer that, my love, as he chose to come this way."

"Oh, it's Daddy's fault is it that we're stuck in ruddy traffic."

"Language Geoffrey."

"Ruddy is not swearing, Marjorie."

"It sounds like it is, so don't do it."

"Why did you choose to get stuck in traffic, Daddy?"

"I didn't choose to, sweetie pie, and contrary to what Mummy said, this is the only route we can use."

"What does contrary mean?"

"It means he is disagreeing with Mummy and Daddy is getting in a paddy because he can't travel as fast as he likes along the motorway."

"I am not getting in a paddy and the problem is not that we not travelling fast, we're not travelling at all. There must be an accident or roadworks."

"It could be just weight of traffic, Geoffrey."

"What's the traffic waiting for, Mummy."

"No, it's not waiting, well it is, but I meant weight, that is it's heavy, there's a lot of it. It's a lot of cars jamming the roads so that nobody can get to where they want to go."

"Why are there a lot of cars?"

"Because, sweetie, today is the first Saturday of the school holidays and as everyone with children has to go on holiday when the schools are shut, everyone has chosen to go on holiday today, so we've all got in our cars at the same time to go to the same place."

"I did suggest setting off earlier, Geoffrey."

"And we would have left earlier if you hadn't forgotten all the things we needed to pack because the cabin we're renting hasn't got half the things we need for a week away from home."

"If you'd read the details of the site sooner, I would have known what to pack."

"We should have booked a cottage which has everything included."

"You said we couldn't afford a holiday cottage."

"Not at the prices they were asking, but you said this cabin thing was just as good."

"Well, it looked very nice in the brochure, with a view over the sea."

"Don't be silly Marjorie. There are probably five hundred cabins in the park. You don't think they'll all have sea views do you."

"Don't call me silly. Not in front of Lily."

"Is Mummy a silly billy, like you are Daddy."

"Who says I'm a silly billy?"

"Mummy did when you banged your head on the back of the car."

"Did she, well, that was a bit silly wasn't it. Let's have a laugh at silly Daddy almost knocking himself out. Ha, ha, ha!"

"Now, now, Geoffrey. You'll scare Lily. We're going on holiday. Let's enjoy ourselves."

"We're not going anywhere at the moment and where we're going, the mattresses will probably be thinner than our ones at home, the duvets meaner, the chairs less comfortable, the TV smaller, you won't be able to cut a loaf of bread because the knives will be blunt, and it will probably be raining, but it won't matter that we can't see the sea because we'll be lost among five hundred other cabins lined up like in a prisoner of war camp."

"If you didn't like the look of this holiday park, Geoffrey, you could have said."

"What else could we do. You've got to take kids on holiday haven't you."

"Daddy, Daddy, the car in front is moving."

"Oh, yes. Well spotted, Lily."

"Are we nearly there yet?"

The Missing Essence – Introduction

This piece was written for a workshop that the writing group held. We each submitted a piece to the tutor on the theme "Earth, Wind and Fire" prior to the workshop. She judged them. I really went to town on the metaphors and description. It seemed to go down well because I won! Incidentally, the workshop focussed on psychic distance - that is, how close the narrator is to the point of view character in a 3rd person story. You can be in their head, on their shoulder or observing from a distance. Where you are determines how much the narrator and hence the reader, can know of the character's thoughts and actions.

The Missing Essence

Pete Earth slung the bass guitar low on his hips, planted his feet a metre apart on the stone floor and strummed a deep chord. Pitched almost too low to be heard by the ears, it thrummed through the ground. Feeling the vibrations through his bones, Ty Wind picked up his Strat and plucked out the notes of a melody that hung in the air like streamers of mist. Spiky ginger-haired, Serena Fire, raised her head and let out a cry that soared like a rocket fizzing to the roof.

The mix of bass rhythm, languid tune and searing treble grew in pace and volume but something was amiss. The timing of Wind's finger-play jarred with Earth's chords and Fire's smouldering lyrics sputtered off key. The track crashed to a conclusion in a chaotic cacophony. Wind felt it like an icy blast from the Arctic, while a tectonic plate scraping past another expressed Earth's discomfort.

Serena turned on her colleagues, cheeks burning.

"Flaming hell, guys. We crashed and burned there. What's up?"

Despite the energy of his playing, Pete's mud-brown hair lay flat on his head. He growled, "We're a rock band. We need a drummer." He nodded to the empty set of drums at the centre of the studio."

Serena flared. "Well, I want to be a star. What are you doing about it, Ty?"

The lead guitarist waved his waved his arms, his fair hair mussed as if by a fierce gale. "I put out a message over the aether," he said.

"Oh, yeah," Serena gave him a glare that could have scorched the bark off a tree. "And what came of that?"

Wind replied breezily, "Actually, I got a reply." He frowned, "I thought she said she would be here by now."

There was a creak as the heavy door of the studio opened. A figure seeped through the gap. She was tall with blue, tight-fitting jeans and a sailor top. She had hair as black as the deepest ocean. It shone with a blue iridescence in the studio lights. Her skin was as white as a frothing waterfall.

"Hi," she said with a voice smooth as the surface of a pond, "I'm Flo, Flo Water. I think you advertised for a drummer."

Wind wafted over the floor to greet her.

"That's right. I'm Ty, short for Typhoon."

"That's what he tells everyone," Earth grunted. "It's Tyson really. Welcome, Flo."

"You say you're a drummer," Serena fired at her, "Let's see you drum."

Flo shrugged and drifted to the set of drums. The others watched as she seemed to fill the space amongst the kit, stretching arms and legs to test her reach. She picked up the sticks and started to tap the snare drum. To the insistent beat, like drips falling from a tap, she added a swish on the cymbal like rain falling on a tin roof. She increased the tempo until with a torrent of limbs she unleashed the sound of a tsunami crashing against a cliff. The roar was enough to stir Earth into tapping a foot. Flo settled into a rhythm of waves breaking on a beach as Pete added rumbling chords that throbbed through the floor. Ty launched a riff resembling a tornado that whirled around the studio and Serena let out a scorching chorus that singed the roof.

The studio filled with sound that shook the walls, each of the musicians contributing their energy. Earth erupted with glowing lava, Fire flickered with flame, Wind grew as hot as a Saharan dust devil and drops of sweat flew off Water's flailing limbs like spray from breakers. As the song reached a crescendo of harmony, all four stopped abruptly on a beat, leaving the reverberations fading away. Serena fell to the floor like a guttering cinder; Flo slumped over the drums like a spent fountain and Ty sagged like a sail without wind. Pete was still.

"Well, I think that says enough," Pete muttered, "we've got all the elements of a band."

All the Stars in the Heavens – Introduction

The theme for this piece was, I recall, "stars". I think the group expected an SF story from me, as usual, but this idea came instead. It's poignant but I felt quite fond of it.

All the Stars in the Heavens

The stars are glowing above me, each with its five, six or seven points, so close I feel I can almost reach out and touch them. That's what they look like, but I know that stars are huge balls of gas giving out light and heat from immense fusion reactions. They are light years apart. But here I am floating, weightless, adrift in space surrounded by them. There's no Sun nearby or planets and the patterns of the stars are not the ones I learned to recognise in pictures. It doesn't matter. I can pick out my own constellations and give them names. There's the cup with a handle of a ring of stars and the cat with a long curving tail. That rectangle of stars looks like a robot and over there, that's a tree.

Space isn't silent but I'm used to the sounds now: the hiss of the air line; the slurp of the pump; the beep-beep of the instrument panel. The cable connects me to the spaceship so I can stay and watch the stars for as long as I wish.

I have been watching them so long that they are starting to fade. Already some have disappeared. I feel sleepy. I am…

The change of tone from the monitor woke her. Instead of the regular pips there was a continuous squeal. It was dark, still night-time. She leapt from the chair. The screens were showing straight lines not regular, reassuring waves. The door swung open. Nurses and a doctor rushed in. They clustered around the bed, peering at the instruments.

She stood at the side looking at the little body under the covers. There was so little left of him now, he was almost weightless. The mask covered his face, tubes and wires linked him to the machines. But his eyes were still open, staring unblinking at the ceiling.

He so loved the stars. He had learned all the regular constellations, Orion, The Great Bear, Cassiopeia. He could point out the stars of his birth sign, Taurus, as well as the other signs of the Zodiac.

The real stars in the sky couldn't be seen from his hospital bed, so they'd put some phosphorescent stickers on the ceiling. Then they added more and more until the walls and ceiling were covered. By day, almost invisible, they absorbed energy from the artificial lighting and from the sunlight streaming through the window. Then at night when the lights were turned off, the blinds closed and the room empty but for him and her, they gave out their pale glow. They seemed to delight him, and he watched them until, before they dimmed, he fell asleep.

Now his eyes were open but unseeing. The machines continued their whine. The medical staff fussed but she knew it was in vain. He had gone from the sickly body that could not be repaired. Maybe, freed from the restrictions of life, he really was floating amongst the stars.

Step – Introduction

The subject of this story on the theme "step" may look like SF but actually I don't think it is. It's more like historical fiction – how things were back in 1969 (who can recall fiddling with the knobs on the back of the TV to get a picture?) with hints of the subsequent nonsensical conspiracy theories.

Step

"That's one small step for a man…"

A breath caught in Ed's throat. The picture on the TV had disappeared in a blizzard of grey and white. The voice was replaced by a noisy hiss.

"No!" Ed cried, leaping from the sofa to kneel in front of the glowing screen. He thumped the top of the wooden cabinet.

"Hey, careful there, lad," father said from the depths of the armchair. "That there's a valuable instrument."

"Valuable! Like heck," Ed moaned. "We've had it years and years, since I was born nearly."

"Nineteen fifty-eight, we bought that television." Ed's dad said, fingering his pipe. "Cost a packet, so look after it."

"But its knackered, Dad, can't you see." Ed gestured to the screen. "The sound's gone too. Just as Armstrong stepped on to the surface. We've missed the most important event of the century."

"I'm not sure about that my boy. I reckon D-day were a might more important than sending a rocket to the Moon. When we got on that beach…"

"Not just a rocket, Dad. Three men. Two of them are there on the Moon."

"Well, 'appen they can go for a walk without you watching 'em."

"But they're sending pictures all the way back to Earth so that everyone can see that they are there, on the Moon, doing it for real."

"Could be Blackpool beach as far as I could make out. The picture's not a lot worse now than it was."

"Yes, it is, Dad. You could see Armstrong coming down the ladder from the LEM. He had one foot on the surface of the Moon. You could see that couldn't you."

Dad shrugged, "Can't say I was paying much attention."

Ed sighed. "But you heard him speak. What was it? One small step."

"Sounded like he was starting to make a speech."

"Well, it was important wasn't it. The first steps of a human on the Moon. The first steps of anyone." Ed paused. "That is. Unless."

"Unless what, lad?"

Ed's eye's opened wide. "Perhaps aliens got there first. Perhaps they've attacked the LEM. That's why we've lost the picture. Maybe Neil Armstrong was killed by aliens before he finished his step."

"What are you rambling about now?" Dad heaved himself out of the sagging chair. "If there's nothing to see I'm going to bed. Time you did too, my lad."

"No. I've got to find out what happened." Ed said, thoughts racing through his head. Perhaps Aldrin and Armstrong had been captured and the aliens had broken the TV link.

"OK, son, but take care with that TV. No more thumping it, do you hear me."

His father left the living room as Ed focussed on the controls at the back of the cubical box. He turned the tuning knob, the vertical hold, the horizontal hold but the picture remained a flickering blur and the sound was that of waves on a pebbly beach.

It had to be the TV that was faulty, surely, but what if it wasn't just this TV. What if no-one could see what was happening in space. What if the astronauts stepping on to the Moon had been met by aliens?

Heels – Introduction

I don't write many stories about my knowledge and experiences of transgender life (except for my Jasmine Frame novels and stories) but the theme "digging my heels in" seemed to beg for it. Apart from a little of the first section nothing of this is autobiographical; I've never even attended a club like the one described, but I have heard accounts of places that are similar. The other thing is that it's written in the second person which I don't try very often.

Heels

You stand in front of the long mirror, turn from side to side, peer at the image. It is not you. Not the you that you see in your mind. You recognise it though, that nose that is too large, the thin lips, the short, thinning hair, the wide shoulders and the narrow hips. It's not all bad. Your new red bra covering the enhancers has given you something of a figure, and the matching knickers are covering what's below.

You sigh and pull on the tights and the red dress. The hem is just above your knee, sexy but not tarty. You sit down at the dressing-table and start applying your make-up. You've done this many times. You know what works and what doesn't. When you're finished you stand and slip the brunette wig onto your head and look in the mirror again. That's better. The wig and make-up may be a disguise, but you are behind it looking out.

You slide your feet into the red shoes with the three-inch, almost-stiletto, heels. You stand again and face the long mirror. You've practised wearing the heels, day after day. You strutted around the flat, holding your head up, forcing your legs and back to be straight. You toppled and almost fell often, but gradually you learnt how to keep your balance and walk while always on tiptoe. It was agony at first, the shoes rubbed your ankles and your toes hurt. It was worth it. Now you're ready.

A beep comes from your phone. You grab it and search out the text message. It's just a smiley but it means that Carol is outside. You glance through the curtain. Yes, there is her car on the road. She's managed to park right by your gate. You put your coat on, the shiny black, pvc mac, and pick up your handbag.

You hurry from the door to the car. It's a dark, damp evening, so perhaps none of the neighbours have seen you, or recognised you.

"Hi, Nikki," Carol says as you slide into the passenger seat. Her voice is lower than yours, but she doesn't care. "Ready for it then?"

"You bet," you reply. Does your nervousness show in your voice? You hope not. You've been looking forward to this evening out. You don't want to appear to be the novice that you really are.

"Let's hit the town then." Carol presses her foot on the accelerator.

The club is crowded. The flashing lights make it almost impossible to discern the variety of bodies, drinking, dancing and chatting, well, shouting at each other. The air is hot and damp and full of smells of cheap perfume, sweat and a few other substances. You sip your g&t while looking around, taking in the sights and the sounds. How many of the girls are like you? How many of the girls are girls? There are men too, some with the girls, some circulating, eyeing up the others, the unattached.

"Let's dance," Carol shouts in your ear. She takes your hand and hauls you up. You stagger a little getting your balance on those three-inch heels. Then you follow her into the mêlée of gyrating bodies. The noise is deafening but there is rhythm. You start to move to the beat, enjoying the feeling of your make-believe breasts oscillating up and down. For a few moments you lose touch with your surroundings, just enjoying being a dancing girl.

Bodies press against you. You open your eyes. A man has inserted himself between you and Carol. He's in a shiny, grey suit with a white shirt and thin black tie. His hair is slicked down and combed to one side. He could be your age, perhaps younger. He's examining you, eyes flicking from the top of your wig down passed your boobs to the hem of your dress which is flapping as you dance.

He gives you a smile. It's not a cheery, friendly smile. It doesn't make you feel happy. He comes closer. It could be the press of the other bodies, but you think it's deliberate. He wants to be close to you. He places a hand on your right hip. You shudder. It wasn't what you were wanting or expecting. What were you expecting? Definitely not contact.

He leans forward so his lips are by your ear.

"Nice dress," he shouts. He straightens up again, the leer back on his face. You try a smile, but you aren't sure if it looks like one.

His hand is still on your hip. You've almost ceased dancing because you're afraid the hand might move with you. He's looking into your eyes. You're looking back. Wondering.

You're not prepared for his next move. His other hand shoots up your dress and grabs you between your legs. He's found something to grab hold of. Now his smile becomes a laugh. His grip tightens. You can't move. You can't think.

He edges forward again, his feet between yours, your crotch held tight. "I thought so. Tranny."

You have to get away. You don't want what he wants, whatever that might be. One thought comes into your brain. You lift your right foot. You slam it down heel first. On his foot.

His hands release you. He falls back. His scream is audible above the music. You stand and stare.

Carol grabs your hand. "Let's get out of here."

She guides you from the club, pausing just to pick up your coats. You're outside.

"Run. Before they see we've gone. He and his mates will do you in if they catch you."

You hurry after her, your heels clattering against the pavement. You're not thinking of keeping your back straight now.

You reach the car. Carol's already inside starting the engine. You move off as you pull the door closed.

You sigh. Carol glances at you as she manoeuvres onto the road and speeds up.

"What did he do? Grab your balls?"

You nod. You're shaking.

"Did you push him or something?"

"I dug my heel into his foot."

Carol laughs.

A question of declination – Introduction

The prompt for this piece of work was a picture, but I can't recall what it was, perhaps a compass or a compass rose. Anyway, somehow it got me onto thinking about declination and the story followed from that. It's a mystery.

A question of declination

"What's this old thing?" Matt said holding up a worn leather case. He undid the straps revealing a slim brass cylinder with a glass face.

"Blimey Charlie," I replied, "I haven't seen that since I was a kid."

"But what is it and what is it doing amongst Grandad's old junk?"

"It's a compass. Let me have a look."

Matt held out the instrument over the heaps of old newspapers, clothes and other assorted detritus of my father's life. I looked at its dull casing, scratched glass and stained card marked with the cardinal directions. The needle didn't turn as I moved the compass.

"It doesn't seem to be working but I remember Dad telling us stories about it, a long time ago."

"What stories?"

I thought back to those days when Dad was always telling tales to excite and enthral his children. Days long gone.

"Well, it's an heirloom; passed down the family for generations. It could be a fairy-tale for all I know, but Dad said that it belonged to a rich man who was an explorer."

"What was our connection with this guy?" Matt asked.

"I think our however-many-times-great grandfather was a servant, a butler or something. The story Dad told was that he was given the compass to look after while the Lord or whatever he was, went off on an expedition to the North Pole, but he never came back. The house was sold off soon after because of debt, so he kept it."

"Well, it's probably the only thing worth anything that Grandad had left."

I looked at the compass again. It wasn't in good condition, but it was certainly antique.

"Perhaps if I clean it up it'll look better and then we can get it valued," I put the compass with my jacket.

A few weeks elapsed sorting Dad's affairs until, one evening, I settled into a chair feeling weary. The compass was on the coffee table where it had been since the day we found it. I decided to take a closer look to see if it was worth selling. I searched for my set of horology tools – the residue of a short-lived hobby. The screws in the bottom plate of the compass were sealed with dirt and old polish but eventually I got them moving. At last, I was able to gently lever the plate off. As I did so a piece of paper fell out. My heart raced. I unfolded the yellow notepaper carefully. A scratchy ink pen had been used but the writing was small and elegant. I stopped breathing and my eyes widened as I read. It was written by George William Fanshawe. It described the whereabouts of a box buried on his estate. A series of compass directions and distances in yards stated the location. I grabbed my mobile and phoned Matt.

"Are you sure it's real?" he asked.

"Why not?" I replied. "It's been in the family for generations. I don't think the back has been taken off for years. It makes sense doesn't it. This Fanshawe bloke was an amateur explorer but knew he was in financial trouble. He hides away his valuables before going off on a trip and entrusts the secret with his trusted servant, well, not quite trusted because he doesn't tell him what's in the compass. Then he goes and dies, and no-one knows."

Matt made some noises of agreement, then said. "Where is it buried? We don't know where this ancestor of ours worked."

"It's on the letter," I shouted, "Fanshawe has written his address at the top of the page - Fanshawe Grange."

"Where's that?"

"I don't know, but you can Google it."

"Hmm, yes, I can. I'll call you back."

Two weeks later we were there – Fanshawe Grange, a National Trust property in the East of England. It was a big Georgian house in a huge, landscaped estate. We examined the map of the area that I had purchased.

Matt said. "Why don't we measure out the directions on the map and save time tramping around the estate."

"I'm not sure the scale is big enough to do that and there's another problem," I replied. "The compass points to the magnetic north pole not true north."

Matt shrugged, "Aren't they the same thing?"

"No, there's a few degrees between where the compass points and true north. It's called declination." I felt proud at remembering my geography lessons from many decades ago.

Matt didn't look impressed. "Okay, we follow the directions then." We went to the steps at the rear of the house where the letter told us to start.

I read the first line of the directions. "West Northwest five hundred yards." I held up my newly purchased compass and found where west northwest was. Then I realised a problem. "How do we measure five hundred yards. We can't just pace it out. It won't be accurate enough."

"I thought of that," Matt replied with a proud grin on his face. He held up his smartphone. "GPS, we can measure how far we walk in any direction."

I stared over the parkland. "Okay, let's go. I'd say five hundred yards will take us into those trees by the lake."

It took us two hours of walking, peering at the compass and the phone screen, and re-reading the letter. We had zig-zagged across the estate until we ended on a slope leading down to a stream, out of sight of the house.

"Hey," said Matt, "Isn't the last instruction, dig under the oak tree facing the sunset?"

"Yes," I said checking the letter. "But there isn't an oak tree here, no tree at all."

"Perhaps it fell down," Matt said.

"Wouldn't they have found the box?"

"Maybe. Perhaps not."

"We'll have to dig to find out," I said, "but not yet. We don't want anyone seeing us."

"I'll record the spot on my app. Then we can come back when the place closes and dig."

We waited out of sight, till evening came. Back at the spot, we dug using the folding spade I brought, along with our picnic, in my rucksack. We made quite a mess of the grass but found nothing.

Back home, I stared at the map. Where had we gone wrong? Had the treasure been discovered long ago? Or maybe there never was any. Matt looked over my shoulder.

"Hey, what do those lines mean?" He was pointing at the key.

"Oh that, it's the magnetic declination. What I told you about."

Matt leaned closer. "It says that this is for July 2016. Does it change?"

"Uh? I don't know."

Matt alternated tapping and staring at his mobile for minute after minute.

"Was there a date on the letter?" he asked at last.

"Yes, 1821." I knew the letter off by heart by then.

"That's it then. The declination has changed by twenty-four degrees since 1821. We were looking in the wrong place."

Next day, we were back at Fanshawe Grange with another picnic and a sheet of paper with all Matt's calculations of the directions that Fanshawe intended when he wrote the letter two centuries ago. This time we ended up by a mature oak tree.

"This looks more like it," Matt said, settling down to relax against the trunk.

The Sun was sinking close to the horizon when we decided it was safe to start digging. The ground was hard and the roots got in the way, but Matt hadn't dug far before he shouted, "There's something here."

We hauled out the small wooden chest. It was only about the size of a shoe box. There was a simple brass catch on the side. No lock. Why bother? The chest had been hidden to keep it safe. I let Matt open the lid. I bent down to look inside. It was lined with lead and divided into compartments like a cash box.

What did I expect? Gold coins, sovereigns; jewellery with diamonds, sapphires and so on; valuables that were compact but easy to sell. What was there in the box? Seeds.

I showed them to a mate who's a botanist. He got excited and identified them as coffee and cocoa beans, seeds of rubber trees, pineapple seeds, passionfruit seeds and other tropical fruits. I worked it out in the end. Fanshawe was an explorer. He'd been to the tropics as well as the Arctic. All his money went into financing his expeditions. What he considered his valuables were the seeds of plants he found on his travels. Plants that produced exotic foods and useful materials. In the early nineteenth century Fanshawe could have made a lot of money from selling those seeds. Not us.

Garden Party – Introduction

From mystery to comedy. This story goes back quite a few years to a writing group meeting which I think had "garden party" as the theme. I just recall it being a hoot to write.

Garden Party

"Canapè, sir?"

"What? Is it going to rain?" Billy looked up at the clear, blue sky, mystified.

There was a drawn-out sigh, "I said, canapé, sir."

Billy noticed the bowtie wearing waiter was holding a tray of doll's house sized burgers in buns.

"Oh, you mean, these. I thought you meant…" Billy nodded towards the marquee occupying the centre of the immaculately trimmed lawn.

"Yes, sir, I know sir. I was referring to these bite-sized, organic rare steaks of Aberdeen Angus beef in an organic whole-meal, sesame seed bun."

"Sounds more than they look," Billy said reaching for a handful.

"One normally eats one at a time, sir."

Billy released the three that were in his left hand but retained the two he was raising to his mouth with his right.

"Oh, of course, got to make them go round, I see."

The waiter sighed again and slid off to a quartet in which the two middle-aged men looked as though they were dressed for a day's sailing and the two mature women wore brightly coloured cocktail dresses.

Billy looked around. Across the lawn between the marquee, swimming pool and the large ivy-clad house were clusters of people similarly smartly dressed. Billy didn't notice them; his eyes had located the waitress carrying a tray of tall glasses emerging from the very large tent. Billy hurried to intercept her.

He skidded to a halt. The glasses rattled as the waitress also stopped suddenly to prevent a collision.

"That's lucky," Billy said.

"What's that, sir?" the girl said, staring at him.

"I can help you with that heavy tray."

"It's alright sir. I was taking it around the guests."

"Oh, in that case, I'll just take a couple." Billy lifted two glasses of the pale, bubbly liquid from the tray. The girl wrinkled her nose, looked sideways at him and then marched off to a group of twenty-somethings in chinos and striped shirts or frilly mini-dresses, depending on gender.

Billy took a sip of the drink. Champagne? It could have been Babycham for all he knew, but it tasted as though it had alcohol in it, so he was happy. He was about to go in search of more of the mini-foods, when a voice in his left ear assaulted him.

"Who are you then?"

Billy turned to see a large, moustache-wielding, ancient in a school tie and striped blazer, leaning on a shooting stick.

"Oh, hi, uh, I'm with, um," Billy searched for a name, "Fiona."

"Fiona? Fiona?" the florid face looked blank, "Oh, Algernon's lass. There she is now." He raised the stick and pointed it to a pair of young women not ten metres away.

"That's right, I'd better get this drink to her."

"But she's already got one."

"Oh, that'll soon be gone. You know Fiona."

"What, oh, yes. Got to keep the filly lubricated, what." The old duffer chortled. Billy made his escape, straight towards the pair of girls.

"Hi, Fiona," Billy said over the girl's shoulder. The girl turned to face him. He fell in love. Her round pale face, large blue eyes, and shiny black hair tied in a pig tail, enraptured him.

"Who are you?"

"I brought you a drink."

"I've got one."

"I thought you might like another."

Fiona looked at the dregs in her glass and smiled. To Billy it was as if the day had been dull and the Sun had just come out.

"Well, thank you. Who did you say you were?"

"Billy."

"Billy? I don't think I know a Billy. Do you, Hettie?" She turned to her companion, a tall blonde with a wide face.

"No. There aren't any cousins called Billy, are there?"

"There aren't. You must be a friend of the family." The girls nodded, convinced they had solved the mystery.

"Yeh, that's right." Billy agreed. Fiona took the glass from his left hand and sipped the champagne. She examined him closely.

"Oh, I do like your jeans and T-shirt. Those rips are so in, aren't they and the streaks of colour. Well, they look almost as if you painted them on yourself." They giggled at the joke.

"Everyone else looks so boring," Fiona continued, "Look at them all."

"Your uncle and aunt's invitation did say it was a Garden Party." Hettie sniffed and smoothed the pleats in her crimson, silk dress.

"Well, I think it's great that someone has decided to be different and rebel a little." Fiona grasped Billy's arm. "Why haven't I met you before, since you're a friend of the family?"

114

"Oh, I've been, um, away for a while."

"Gap?"

"There was a bit in between..."

"I'm going to South America on mine. Hettie's coming too." Hettie nodded.

"Let's go and find some more finger-food," Fiona went on.

After a shot glass of gazpacho, a minute triangle of bread with a spot of patè de foie gras, and a biscuit with a single prawn, Billy was feeling in need of something more substantial.

"When will they serve the real food?" he asked.

"Real food?" Fiona giggled.

"Yeh, proper sized portions."

"Oh, you won't get any of that this afternoon. As Hettie said, it's a garden party."

"Really, I think I need something more. It takes more energy chasing around trying to catch the waiters than you get from these mini bites."

"Oh, you are funny. Look there's Aunt Deborah. I'm sure she'd like to say hello."

A horsy woman in a tweed skirt was striding across the lawn from the house.

"No, she looks busy." Billy tried to tug Fiona in direction perpendicular to Aunt Deborah's determinedly straight path.

"She's coming straight towards us. Hello, Aunt Deborah,"

"What's he doing here?" Aunt Deborah pointed a finger at Billy.

"That's Billy, a friend of the family," Fiona said innocently.

"Friend of the family, my foot," Aunt Deborah roared, "He's painting the downstairs loo Christmas hyacinth blue. I'm not paying you to drink my champagne. Shoo."

Parallel Parking – Introduction

A much more recent example this. The topic was "car park", not the most interesting of themes. Could I make a romance of it? Well, could I?

Parallel Parking

I was never very good at parallel parking. For my third driving test the kindly examiner presented me with a long stretch of kerb to park against and I managed to draw up alongside it to his satisfaction, just. My ex-husband always scoffed that women can't park. "There's always a wheel on the pavement or the bumper sticking out into the traffic," so he said. That from a man who was blind to speed limit signs. He accrued so many penalty points that he lost his licence just before we divorced. The settlement gave me enough money to buy myself a new car. I chose one that had automatic parking assist.

One day, I drove into town to do a spot of window shopping. The side roads were lined with cars, but I found a gap big enough for my car to park in. I pressed the APA button, lifted my foot off the pedals and took my hands off the steering wheel. The car began to move slowly. I pulled down the sun-visor and peered into the vanity mirror. I was applying my lipstick when the car jerked to a halt with a frantic beeping.

I looked through the windscreen. My car and another that looked very similar were each wedged into the parking space at an acute angle. The driver of the other car got out and approached. I lowered my window.

He appeared to be a little younger than me and pretty dishy. He leaned to speak to me.

"I am sorry. Our cars seem to have arrived at an impasse. I'll reverse and go to another space. I think one has just appeared up the road."

He did as he promised. Once his car had moved my car resumed its methodical and smooth parking. I completed my cosmetic refinements and got out. As I was locking my car, the man reappeared.

"I must apologise for that little contretemps," he said. I liked his tone. "I'm dreadful at parking and just let my car do the job. I'm sorry that we chose the same spot."

Golly, a man who admits to being bad at some aspect of driving. I was drawn to him.

He went on, "Perhaps I can buy you a coffee." He seemed to imply it as some sort of recompense for the inconvenience. I was in no rush and a coffee was probably top of my priorities anyway, so I accepted.

We bonded over the cappuccino (mine) and latte (his). We shared stories of parking disasters and were soon laughing at each other's tales. Long after our cups had been emptied, we arranged a date for the following evening.

The meeting place was a vast, spacious carpark. We parked our cars in adjacent slots. They weren't quite parallel.

Pretty Woman – Introduction

Why we chose "Pretty Woman" as a theme I cannot remember but it evoked memories of the Roy Orbison song and the film starring Julia Roberts and Richard Gere. My thoughts followed a different route. They arrived at a story with some elements resembling one or two other stories and a scene from my first Jasmine Frame novel. Nevertheless, the story is original and again, non-autobiographical. The group found it quite moving.

Pretty Woman

"I am pretty," she said aloud. She repeated it often as an affirmation. In her mind's eye it was true, she was a pretty woman. The mirror rendered her self-image a lie. She saw a gangly and shapeless figure. Her chin jutted and her large nose dominated her face. She didn't look in the mirror often. Despite her anxiety she had been persuaded to go out with friends, well, people she knew. They were going clubbing.

She'd bought a new dress that delighted her. Cobalt blue with a pattern in black and white that disrupted the shape like wartime camouflage. It was short enough to display her long, shapely legs, but long enough not to cause embarrassment. It fitted where it should but covered her lumpy bits and had a bare shoulder and arm that completed the dramatic effect.

The day was spent getting ready. She bathed, and shaved and moisturised and perfumed her body before dressing in her best lingerie. Never stint on underwear, she'd been told. Then she put on the dress and finally spent a long time on her make-up. She risked a look in the mirror and was quite pleased with what she saw. There was an attractively dressed woman. Pretty? It was a work in progress.

She arrived fashionably late at the club but so had everyone else. The DJ was struggling to generate an atmosphere on the empty dance floor. She joined the first arrivers at the bar and met a couple she knew. Once a couple of Proseccos had been downed the place was filling up. It was time to join the dancers.

Soon she was lost in the rhythm of the drum and bass, the music drowning out all attempts at conversation and she felt the heat of bodies around her. When she next opened her eyes, she saw that a man was dancing close to her. He wore a white t-shirt stretched over a muscley torso and tight, blue jeans which emphasised the bulge at his crotch. He gave a half-smile when he saw her looking at him and moved closer. The press of bodies prevented her from maintaining distance. He mouthed something. His lips might have said "pretty woman", but she wasn't sure. It could have been something else. His arm reached out around her waist and the palm of his hand pressed against her bum. He pulled her closer to him and his crotch pressed against her.

The beat changed, a slower track. He tugged on her bottom, pulling her to the edge of the dance floor. Then he gave her a gentle shove along a corridor.

He wants to go somewhere quieter, she thought, somewhere where we can talk. There was a touch of anxiety about leaving the people she knew, but there was a thrill of feeling that he found her attractive enough to want to get to know her.

She became a little concerned as they passed the quiet rooms and moved further along the narrow, dark corridor. There was only a fire door ahead.

He pushed her against the door and released the catch. The door swung open. She stumbled into a dark, cold, litter-strewn alley, struggling to find balance on her heels.

"Trannie!" he mumbled as his arm swung. The fist landed on her chin. The second caught her cheek as she fell. Then he was kicking and leaning over her to land more punches.

"Shame about your dress. It's very smart," the nurse said, dabbing at her bleeding lip. The dress was torn and bloodied like her face. Every breath hurt because of the bruised ribs and there was a pain in her groin. She was thankful that some of her new friends had followed her to the alley. Her assailant had run away. She wondered whether she'd ever feel confident about going clubbing or even leaving the house again.

"Don't worry love," the nurse went on. She looked into her eyes and smiled. "It looks worse than it is. It'll heal and you'll soon be a pretty woman again."

The Accident – Introduction

And lastly, a real short, short. This was written mid-Covid-lockdown, the first one. Need I say more.

The Accident

Where was why? Oh, yes, telling you about the accident. There I was just hanging out in this or that cell and merrily copying myself over and over again. Now and again, I'd take to the air and float off to another bat and do the same thing some more. Well, this time, the one I'm telling you about, just by chance there was another one in the cell, not quite the same as me. He had a few different shaped spikes on him. We got chatting as you do and swapped a few bases here and there. That was it, he went off to copy himself and so did I. The new stuff this other fellow gave me was really useful. I multiplied lots of times and then set off for pastures new. I came across a human. I hadn't bothered with them before but now I felt like a change and with my new bits I knew I had the means. I latched onto a cell in his lungs and with a bit of twisting I was in. There before me was the nucleus and the bundle of lovely DNA. I had a real party and, in no time at all, there were thousands, millions, billions of me. We set out to find other humans and the rest, well you know…

The Tales of Agent Kappa

Agent Kappa is a British secret agent, somewhere between James Bond and Johnny English. Spy stories are, I suppose, a sub-genre of thrillers. Most of them do have a science feel although I do not consider them to be science fiction. Unlike the other stories in this collection, the prompts were not suggested by my writing groups but the results were shared with them.

Propelled to Glory – Introduction

This story was written as a competition entry. The prompt was that a particular object had to be included. I think you will be able to guess what it was. The story didn't appeal to the judge, perhaps because they reported that the "best" stories are those where the reader forgets the prompt. I'm not sure that I agree but there we are. The judge's opinion is final and there are no doubt other reasons why it wasn't shortlisted.

It wasn't the first Agent Kappa story to be written but I think it is suitable to be the first here.

Propelled to Glory

"This is a matter of grave importance." The Boss' statement brought no reaction from Agent Kappa's bushy eyebrows. "The enemy have embarked on a new offensive in the cyberwar. It is not just the fake news and attacks on our systems but the mind-sapping pap they feed our citizens. But we can retaliate if we get you into one of their facilities."

His right eyebrow rose a millimetre. "You want me to destroy it."

The Boss smiled. "No, Kappa, something better. You are going to subvert it."

Kappa frowned. He did not know what she meant. That wasn't unusual. "Can't we do that from here? Hack them or something."

"No. Their processers and servers are behind several firewalls. However, our friends can get you into the complex. Security checks will be extreme. No electronic gadgets at all."

"Nothing?"

124

"Nothing at all. No phones, watches, smart glasses, and no guns either."

Kappa couldn't imagine going on a mission without his usual kit.

"All you will have with you, Kappa is this." She opened a drawer of her desk and took out a slim box. She pushed it towards him. It was leather covered and reminded him of the case of a fountain pen and pencil set he was given for Christmas as a child. He opened the lid. There indeed was a pencil. It was gold, with engraved curlicues and spirals.

"It looks like a Sampson Mordan, but I don't recognise the design."

The Boss nodded. "I didn't know you were so knowledgeable about stationery, Kappa, but yes, it is modelled on Mordan's designs. The gold will stop X-ray penetration and it is operated entirely by springs. The tech department will explain how it works and operations will give you the full briefing. Good luck."

Kappa knew that was the end of the interview. He took the pencil from its case and slipped it into the inside pocket of his Saville Row jacket.

Kappa slipped through the door as it slid open and ducked behind a metal tower. The sole occupant of the vast cavern, seated at a terminal a dozen metres away turned, looked at the closing doors of the lift, shrugged and returned to staring at his screen.

The Boss had been right about the security. He'd been stripped, searched, sniffed, scanned and irradiated, but he'd got through it all. Here he was at the core of the facility and he still had the gold propelling pencil in his pocket.

Kappa peered over the cabinet. It was one of many lined up in rows that disappeared into the gloom. Some housed processing units and servers, most were memory banks while others contained pumps and heat exchangers that prevented the vast computing complex from overheating. None of that meant much to Kappa. The huge space was filled with a soft low hum and a higher pitched whine. It was lit only by the multi-coloured LEDs on the cabinets except for the lamp illuminating the operative's desk. Kappa took the propelling pencil from his pocket and fingered the gold filigree. He knew exactly where to press.

With rubber soles silent on the marble floor, he crept towards the computer operator, pencil held like a dagger. Kappa was behind him before the seated man reacted. Perhaps he saw Kappa's reflection in the screen because the computer technician started to turn. Kappa lunged, pressing the point of the pencil into the short-haired man's neck. He pressed the concealed button and the 0.8mm diameter, 4 cm long graphite tube slid forward piercing the skin and releasing its cargo of nerve agent. The man's breathing stopped mid-gasp; his expression frozen in a look of horror. Every muscle in his body contracted as his neurones fired for the last time. The body curled and toppled from the chair.

Kappa took his place. He thumbed the pencil again. The diamond-tipped carbon-composite drill bit slid out and, silently spinning, drilled a 1mm hole in the workstation casing. He felt the drill head reach empty space and withdrew it. He selected another of the "leads" and pushed the graphite rod through the hole. Kappa had no knowledge of what happened next, but inside the computer the rod, a rolled-up sheet of doped graphene, unwound and settled over the processor. Connections were made and the newly installed circuitry began its task, piggybacking on the computer's own hardware. Messages began to be sent to the AI inhabiting the banks of processors in the cabinets in the room, new data inserted into memories, algorithms amended. Within nano-seconds new messages were appearing on social media accounts around the world, each with a subtly altered emphasis.

Agent Kappa rose, his job done. He was just the delivery man, disposable. It was up to him if he was to be reused, recycled or just reduced to landfill. Getting out would be more difficult than getting in but he still had a few leads in his pencil. The first step was to gain time. Removing, or rather, concealing the body was imperative, then if another of the enemy came down in the lift and found the desk unmanned, they would think the operator was just inspecting one of the countless banks of IT equipment.

He dragged the body across the smooth floor till he reached the rough wall of the natural cave. He looked around. The spot was out of sight of the lift and the desk. It would be unlucky if the next person on site looked here first.

Now for his escape. He'd already chosen his route, the ventilation shafts. It was always the ventilation shaft. He reckoned he was an expert on air quality maintenance systems and there was nothing unusual about the setup at this facility. The clip of the pencil worked as a screwdriver to loosen the grill. He climbed into the tube. Now he had to delay pursuers. Once again, the pencil came to his aid. He pressed the rubber on the top of the pencil to the frame of the lift. The pressure turned it into a gel which he dabbed on both sides of the entrance to the shaft. Then he selected another lead. He pressed the point into the gel then slowly carried the pencil across the diameter of the tube. A unimolecular carbon fibre that had been coiled up to form the lead, unravelled. The gel quickly hardened securing the nanometre thick wire. Kappa didn't wait to see if the tripwire was successful. He began crawling along the pipe. He had to assume that the first person to follow him would find themselves sliced like a lump of cheese.

He emerged on the mountainside. It was dusk. Kappa moved from shrub to bush, feeling his way down. He paused. A figure was standing on the route he needed to take, a figure he recognised. A twig snapped under his foot. He was immediately bathed in light from the torch the figure held.

"Ah, Agent Kappa, at last. I thought you'd take this route."

A feeling of inevitability came over Kappa. "General Balakin, we meet again." Kappa took a few slow, careful paces towards the light, taking the pencil from his pocket and holding it in his hand while feeling for one of the concealed buttons. "Standing guard duty is somewhat beneath you, General."

"I wanted to be present at your final demise, Kappa."

Through the bright light, Kappa could see that his enemy held a pistol pointing at him.

"My demise, General?" At a range of no more than five metres he aimed the pencil and pressed the button. The four-centimetre rockette launched. Briefly Kappa saw a pinhead of flame as it expended the fuel stored in its graphene tube shaft. Balakin dropped the torch and slapped his cheek as if attacked by a mosquito. Then he froze and collapsed as the neurotoxin in the tip of the micro-missile took effect.

Kappa stepped over the body and hurried to the one-man quadcopter which had been hidden beneath greenery. He pulled the camouflage from it and opened the cockpit cover. Settling himself into the seat he flicked the engines on. The electric fans powered by the lithium-sulfur batteries started up with a faint hum. There was one last diversion to arrange before closing the cockpit. He aimed the pencil over the undergrowth and fired another rockette. After a short trajectory the missile broke up into millions of carbon-60 bucky balls. Air resistance heated them until they burst releasing their cargo of fluorine oxide. Kappa watched the brief and tiny but fiercely hot fireball ignite the tinder dry vegetation. He slipped the pencil back into his inside pocket then took off silently as the brush fire took hold.

He kept low, following the contours until he reached the coast, then headed out into the ocean. The submarine would be a few miles offshore. There he could relax, mission over, and bask in the glory. There might even be a message of congratulation from the Boss, but she would demand a report. Would she accept it written in pencil?

Getting the Message – Introduction

The prompt for this story was an article I read in New Scientist Magazine. First and foremost it is a spy story featuring Agent Kappa but there is a sciency context. Nevertheless, I don't consider it to be science fiction. You can make your own mind up.

Getting the Message

Agent Kappa hunched over the small glass of the fiery spirit. It was an acquired taste which he had acquired to look like a local. He tugged the threadbare overcoat around his shoulders. The bar was cold, dim and dingy like most of the establishments in this town. Its windows onto the grey street were crusted with greasy grime and cracked, just like the dull brown floor tiles. Anywhere else, he may have stood out, but here there were at least half a dozen similarly attired men, he presumed they were men, sitting alone contemplating their glasses with varying degrees of moroseness.

Kappa sighed. Another mission which had gone off the rails. He did not know why he was here, and his contact had failed to appear. While the implant located in his groin may have been sending encrypted data about his physical state, location and his senses, he dared not ask for information to be beamed to him. He was effectively on his own, but he had no idea what he was expected to do now.

He kept his head down, looking as despondent as his fellow drinkers, but kept watch from his table close to the door. When it creaked open, he didn't move. A man limped through the entrance, leaning heavily on the doorhandle. He had no overcoat to fend off the freezing rain, just a soaked woollen jacket. He took one step into the café, staggered another, dripping rainwater tinged with the red of blood onto the tiles. He took three more short, foot dragging steps towards Kappa.

Was it the man Kappa had been expecting? It could be, but his dishevelled appearance barely matched the image that Kappa had in his memory. More bodies crowded the doorway wearing smart waterproof macs. Their appearance indicated that they were the, definitely-not-secret, internal security police. Kappa tensed. His false identity may be insufficient to protect him from close scrutiny.

One of the police raised a hand holding a gun that was bigger than it needed to be. The shot rattled the windows and the bottles behind the bar. The man cried out and slumped across Kappa's table. His left hand reached out to Kappa, briefly gripping the lapel of his coat, then slid down his chest to hang limp.

Kappa rose as did half the other men in the bar. Perhaps they weren't depressed locals after all. He shoved the body of the man off the table into the path of the advancing police. Turning, he pushed passed his fellow drinkers lurching towards him. He rushed to the back of the bar.

He had prepared for such an escape, of course, and knew the route through the storeroom and backyard into the network of narrow lanes and alleyways that threaded through the neighbourhood.

Sounds of pursuit were lost in the pitter-patter of rain falling on the roofs and pavements. Kappa was sure he had escaped his pursuers for now. He slipped into another yard and paused to tear the silicone film from his face and hands. He popped the thin contact lenses from his eyeballs. Now his fingerprints, iris pattern and skin tone matched another person entirely. He dropped the id card and papers of his previous identity into a rubbish bin, pulled his coat tight around him and set off at a fast but relaxed walk. This mission was over, now all he had to do was get out of this hole of a country.

"Good morning, Agent Kappa. Sit down, please." The Boss spoke in her usual calm and soothingly pleasant voice. Kappa placed himself in the only chair that was available that faced her desk. He was somewhat surprised at the Boss' cheerful manner. Surely the mission had been a failure.

"Well done. Kappa, it is good to see you again looking so fit and well."

"Well, done? As far as I know I did nothing."

"You met your contact, did you not?" The Boss was giving him the knowing grin that suggested that she knew something he didn't.

"I wouldn't say met. If he was my intended informant, he was dead when he fell across my table. We didn't say a word to each other."

"But you touched."

Kappa had to think for a moment. Yes, the man had reached out to grasp his overcoat.

"His hand did touch me, but that was all."

"It was enough, Kappa. You got away with it."

"I did?" He was completely bemused by the Boss' bonhomie.

"Yes, though it was a bit of luck that you were still wearing that old coat when you got back."

He had considered dumping it, but it had been his only protection from the cold and the wet. Light began to dawn. "You mean the contact left something attached to it."

"Correct, Kappa. Come with me." The Boss rose from her seat and lead him from the office. They descended into the depths of HQ and entered one of the many brightly lit laboratories. Amongst the benches and white-cased machines, Kappa noticed an evidence bag containing the old grey overcoat. They were approached by a young blonde woman in a white coat.

"Welcome to Lab 121 Dame Tillington. How can I help you?"

The Boss gave her broad smile. "I've brought Agent Kappa here, for you to explain why, for once, his mission wasn't the disaster he thought." She turned to Kappa, "Dr Crowfoot is one of our brightest young scientists."

The woman seemed to glow with a mixture of pride and embarrassment. "Of course,' she said, tapping a keyboard. "All the clothing you were wearing on your return was given the routine search. We found this under the lapel of your overcoat. It fluoresced when illuminated with a particular frequency of uv light." She pointed to a display. Kappa saw a slim grey rectangle not unlike a credit card.

"I'm sure I would have noticed the contact shoving that on me," he said.

"Oh, I doubt it." Dr Crowfoot said, "This is a magnified image. The actual piece of plastic was only 2 by 3 millimetres. It was lucky that it caught under the threads of your lapel."

Dame Tillington, "It was even luckier that the dying man was able to transfer it to you."

Kappa was bemused. "But what is it?"

The scientist smiled at him. "I suppose you could call it a data card."

"That small?" Kappa said, "How much data can it hold?"

"A few terabytes," Dr Crowfoot said.

Kappa was not convinced. "How? I passed through various surveillance machines getting out of the country. They would have detected any metal or electronic circuitry."

The young woman shook her head. "No, none of that. It is simply a piece of polymer impregnated with a variety of special molecules."

"Molecules?"

"Yes, carbon, hydrogen, oxygen and nitrogen atoms bonded together in various structures. We just had to extract and analyse them."

"How?" Kappa asked finding himself intrigued.

"The chip was vaporised and the gases passed through a mass spectrometer to identify the structure of the molecules," Dr Crowfoot continued pointing to another screen that was part of a larger piece of kit. Kappa peered at the display of spikes.

"What does that tell you?"

"Not a lot but the computer is programmed with the same hexadecimal code as the arrangement of the atoms. It provides a readout of the text, numerical data, images and so on, stored in the molecules at a nanometre scale. Hence why so much can be packed onto a tiny substrate."

Kappa nodded with approval. "So, what information did that dying fellow pass on to me. Plans for weapons, troop movements…"

"Nothing like that," the Boss interrupted.

"What then?" Kappa said, bemusement returning.

"The social media entries for the last six months of all the members of the ruling council."

"Social media!"

"Yes," Dame Tillington grinned. "We have evidence of enough bribes and sexual improprieties to bring down the entire government or at least extort them into following our instructions. They won't get away with anything."

Reference

"*Jane Austen quote stored in molecules*" p.19 New Scientist 1 May 2021 No.3332

Imposter – Introduction

This was actually the first Agent Kappa story that I wrote. It was prompted by an article I read – yes, of course, in the *New Scientist.* Again though, I don't consider it a science fiction story even though the present day science provides the plot.

Imposter

"Right, team. Subject has left the building. You're clear to go," Agent Tau watched the feeds from the vids on the three operatives as they entered the building. Their syncopated breathing came over the sound pick-ups. Each was in an isolation suit fed air from oxygen tanks on their back, their exhaled breath captured. They moved swiftly into the hotel bedroom, removed the bedding, and packed it into plastic bags which were then sealed. One traversed the carpet with a high-vacuum collector while the other two swabbed every surface, including walls, ceiling and windows. Then they moved into the bathroom and repeated their actions including removing faeces from the trap previously placed in the waste system. Tau said nothing as they performed the task as planned but she kept an eye on the clock.

The lead operative raised a thumb.

"OK, guys. Get out of there," Tau said, satisfied with what she had seen. She watched as the trio left the room and exited the hotel by the service stairs and door. Soon they were aboard their van and Tau let out the breath she found she was holding.

"Good work. Get back to HQ. Let's see if we've got what the meds wanted."

"Come in Kappa. Delighted you could make it."

Agent Kappa stepped into the Boss' office, placing each foot carefully, eyes searching the room and its occupant for anything out of place. This was home but you could never let your guard drop. To the Boss he appeared to saunter into the room looking relaxed and calm. Kappa was good at creating false impressions. It was what spies did.

The Boss indicated a chair on the other side of her desk. Kappa sat down, testing the strength of the arms and legs before trusting it with his weight. He slouched.

"I have a job for you Kappa," the Boss said. Kappa shrugged. Why else would he be here. "It's a regime change, an assassination."

Kappa raised his eyebrows. "Isn't that more Beta's line of work. Direct action, guns and explosions, that kind of thing. I'm usually the undercover surveillance sort of operative."

"That's true." The Boss nodded her head. "This operation uses your skills but there is, as you say, a bit of direct action." She flicked a finger. An image appeared in the air a few inches from the wall on Kappa's left. "Do you know this person."

Kappa examined the two-dimensional representation. He recognised it alright. It could have been himself, but he noted the minor differences – the particular shade of brown of the hair, the precise fall of the fringe, the two millimetres between the eyes more than his own.

"Yes, It's Dmitri Borodin, right hand man of President-for-life Gagarovich of the former Soviet republic of Rusbenya."

"Correct Kappa."

"Is he the target?"

"No. For obvious reasons he is the one you are going impersonate. The target is the President's son, Vitaly, his named successor."

"Gagarovich has been in power for over forty years," Kappa commented.

"Yes, and a thorn in our flesh for all that time, but he's dying. Reports say he has had at least one stroke. Nevertheless, he's still hanging on and hasn't yet ceded power to Vitaly."

"So, you want me to remove the son before he steps into his father's shoes and makes things even worse."

"That's right."

"I return to my first observation. Isn't that a job for Beta. He could take out Vitaly without missing a sip of his cocktail."

The boss smiled. "I detect a certain disdain for your fellow agent, Kappa, or is it because you're teetotal?"

Kappa shook his head, "He likes the action. I don't. Why do you need me?"

"You must make it look like Borodin, the loyal fixer, has done the deed. That way we remove the whole top strata of Gagarovich's regime. When he dies, we can get a more amenable character in his place."

Kappa felt doubtful. "You want me to take Borodin's place and kill Vitaly. It will be difficult to make it convincing. With all the technical support Gagarovich gets from his friends, they'll soon find out it was an imposter who did the job.'

The Boss nodded, "Which is why we need to prepare you very carefully for this operation Kappa. You will be replacing the real Borodin more thoroughly than you can imagine."

For once Kappa found himself without a response. The boss looked towards the door and said, "Send in Agent Tau."

Kappa turned as the door opened. He hadn't met Agent Tau before, but he had heard reports and respected her for her talents. He stood up and nodded a greeting to the woman entering the room.

"Hello, Kappa," Tau said, "Delighted to meet you at last."

"And me, you," Kappa responded.

"That's enough small talk," the Boss said. "Take Kappa to the medical suite, please Tau, and get him ready. You can explain the procedures if you like."

"Procedures?" Kappa said, feeling somewhat out of the picture.

"You have nineteen days to prepare to be Borodin. That's as far ahead we can predict his movements and that of young Gagarovich."

"I don't usually need that long to prepare," Kappa said.

"This is a special operation, Kappa. You have to become Borodin in order to evade the Rusbenya identity checks both before and after the operation."

Kappa shrugged.

"Come on, Kappa. The medical team are waiting," Tau said. Still bemused, Kappa followed her from the office.

Kappa didn't feel well, in fact, he thought, he didn't feel himself, which was probably quite true. Since arriving in the medical wing, he had been stripped, showered, scrubbed and showered again with what felt like caustic soda, then fed pills that made him shit like his whole insides were falling out. He hadn't eaten a thing for two days but had been on an intravenous drip to keep his energy levels normal and his mind alert.

Now he was lying on his front, naked, with a finger up his backside.

"The faecal implant is in place," The owner of the finger said, her voice muffled by her mask. "The microbes should repopulate your alimentary system in a few days." The finger withdrew as did the medical team. A nurse, also dressed in full sterile kit, laid a sheet over his bare buttocks, and told him to lie still for a while.

"How are you doing, Kappa," Agent Tau said, appearing in 3-D miniature just in Kappa's field of view.

"Perhaps you can explain now what this has to do with me impersonating Dmitri Borodin," Kappa said not a little aggrieved.

"Haven't you worked it out yet, Kappa," Tau said with a hint of a chuckle.

"No."

"You have to be Borodin in every way. You already look pretty much like him but to satisfy their surveillance and the forensic examination that will take place after you kill young Gagarovich, you must have the presence of Borodin."

"The presence?"

"Yes. It must appear that it was Borodin in the room where the young man is killed, and in other parts of the palace."

"So, what's with the anal exploration?"

"We've changed your microbiome, Kappa."

"My mike-what?"

"The several kilograms of microbes that you carry on and in you. The washing procedure removed the bugs from your skin and the laxatives and antibiotics that you've taken killed off the ones in your gut. Now we've replaced your inner microbes with Borodin's."

"I've got Borodin's bugs in me!"

"Yes. We were lucky. Borodin visited London for a trade conference a few weeks ago. We stripped the room he stayed in of all his detritus, sloughed off skin, faeces, semen, yes, he wanked a few times, and the cloud of microbes that we leave behind wherever we go."

"I think I'm beginning to follow this."

"Good. We've cultured the mix of microbes we collected and they're now sitting in your gut. Your insides are now the same as Borodin's."

"How will that help?'

"When the forensics people go in after you kill the son, they'll do a sweep of the room and will detect Borodin's microbe signature not yours."

"But what about my DNA. Won't I be dropping cells here, there and everywhere. I can't do the operation wearing an isolation suit."

"That's where the next procedure comes in."

"What procedure?"

"Wait and see. Sweet dreams."

Kappa looked at his hands, examining each finger and the lines on each palm. He thought he knew his hands, but these weren't his. The fingerprints were different. His life-line didn't stretch as far as it used to. He raised a hand to his cheek.

"Don't touch," the doctor said. "The culture needs some time to, er, set."

"Just relax and enjoy the rest," Agent Tau said from somewhere behind his head. He was suspended about a millimetre above the smooth flat metallic surface; the back of his legs and torso covered in a sprinkling of superconducting-ceramic magnets, repelling the surface so that no part of his body touched it.

"What have you done to me?" Kappa asked.

"Given you Borodin's skin," Tau replied. "Actually, it's partly his skin and partly a synthetic polymer. We cultured the cells and the skin bacteria and fungi we found in

141

Borodin's room then impregnated the polymer. It covers your own skin to a depth of about one hundred microns. It's permeable of course so your own skin can live normally but none of your skin cells will fall off. You'll shed a trickle of Borodin's skin cells and microbes wherever you go."

"So, DNA and microbe tests will show that Borodin has been present and not me."

"That's right. We haven't got long though. The new skin will wear off in about ten days."

Kappa did a quick count. "That's only two days after the mission is due to end."

"That's right. We have to get you in and out pretty quickly. But you've got a week for your insides and outsides to settle. Oh, and to fit contacts so you can get through the iris i.d."

Kappa looked at his hands again. "I presume I've got Borodin's fingerprints?"

"That's right. The polymer skin is imprinted with them."

"I'm not me at all anymore, am I," Kappa said.

"Not to any sensors, you're not."

"I'd better make sure I behave like Borodin then."

"I gather he's a misogynistic brute who delights in violence."

Kappa snorted, "With a taste for western fast food and vodka."

"You're going to have to adjust a fair bit then aren't you, Kappa," Tau said.

The door was held open for him as he left the palace. The rear door of the stretched Mercedes was opened by the armed guard who stood to attention and saluted him. Kappa eased himself into the seat.

"Good to see you again, Comrade Borodin," the driver said, looking in his mirror. "Where can I take you."

"Into town," Kappa said, "The Peacock Club."

The driver nodded, "Of course."

They drove off slowly, passing through the fortified gates of the palace compound. Soldiers saluted and Kappa graciously waved to them. He allowed himself to relax just a little. The job was done. The kid was dead, and he had got out without the alarm being raised, yet.

The electric limousine sped away into the sparse traffic, ignoring speed limits. After all, the passenger was a senior member of the government; laws didn't apply to him. Now all that remained was to get out of the country and leave the real Borodin to face the music.

It wasn't long before they were driving down the narrow streets of the old town. Old neon lights flickered from doorways offering food, drinks and sex in a variety of tastes. The car drew up at the entrance to one such with a peacock's tail flashing above the entrance.

"No need to wait for me," Kappa said as he got out. The driver nodded, closed the door and resumed his driving seat. He drove off before Kappa entered the club.

He was recognised at once, the staff and the manager bowing and offering anything he wanted.

"Vodka," Kappa ordered, surprised that he actually meant it. He felt an urgent need for the alcoholic hit, "and food, my usual," he added.

He was led to a private booth out of sight of the rest of the clientele. A waitress in a very short skirt and low-cut blouse brought him a small glass and a bottle of vodka. If she had been seen on the street dressed like she was here in the club, Kappa knew she would have been assaulted or arrested. Probably both and not necessarily in that order. He felt a strange emotion. His hand reached out and touched her bare

143

thigh. Her leg trembled. He snatched his hand away. She filled the glass, smiled at him, and withdrew.

He glanced at the Rolex watch on his wrist. Five minutes to his pick-up. Time for a couple of drinks. He threw the vodka down his throat. The burning sensation had shocked him at first but now a feeling of satisfaction filled him. He poured another glass.

A minute or two passed and the alcoholic glow permeated him. The waitress returned with a plate that she placed in front of him. American style hamburger and fries. He gave her a wink. She smiled again and left him to eat.

A small light flickered faintly on his watch. His transport had arrived. Well, they can wait a moment, can't they, Kappa thought. He lifted the burger in its bun to his mouth and took a bite. He followed it with a handful of fries.

"Where are you, Kappa? We're outside." Tau said in his ear.

Kappa growled and looked at the burger wistfully. Bloody woman, ordering him about. He imagined doing certain violent things to her.

"Come on, Kappa. Get rid of the gun and get out."

Kappa remembered he still had the murder weapon in his pocket. He didn't want to be caught with it. He'd better join Agent Tau. He took the gun from his jacket, dropped it gently under the seat, knocked back the glass of vodka and got up. He didn't feel quite steady on his feet. He started to head back towards the front entrance then remembered. It was at the rear of the club that Tau was waiting. He staggered towards the toilets.

He emerged blinking into the bright light and hot, humid air. A Toyota taxi waited with its rear door open. He stumbled towards it and fell into the back seat.

"Close the door, Kappa. Let's go."

144

Kappa pulled the door closed and immediately the car drew away. "Don't you go telling me what to do, Tau."

"What kept you, Kappa?" Tau asked.

"Just a full bottle and a burger," Kappa said.

"What? You kept us waiting while you ate and drank. Are you out of your mind, Kappa?"

Kappa slapped her. "Shut up, you slut. No woman tells Agent Kappa what to do."

Tau felt her bruised cheek. "We thought this might happen. Sorry Kappa." She drew a gun from under her leg and shot him.

Kappa woke up. He was in a bed; the surroundings looked familiar; the medical wing that he'd spent a couple of weeks in before the mission. Agent Tau stood by his side.

"Ah, you're awake. Good. How are you feeling Kappa?"

Kappa wasn't sure how to answer. He felt as if he'd been ill and was recovering, as if he'd had a bout of diarrhoea or flu.

"Not wonderful. Why?"

"No uncontrollable urges for alcoholic beverages or processed foods?"

"Uh? No."

"Good. The replacement of your microbiome was successful then. We kept you out for a few days for your own good. You are completely yourself again, Agent Kappa."

"Um, thank you. The mission?"

"The boss has declared it an almost complete success," Tau said, smiling broadly. "Dmitri Borodin has been arrested, tried and executed for the murder of the President-elect."

"Executed, already?"

"Justice is swift in Rusbenya, Kappa, and the weight of the DNA and microbe cloud evidence against him was unarguable. He had no way of proving that he wasn't in the Presidential Palace when Vitaly was killed, or in the Peacock Club where the murder weapon was found. President Gagarovich is in a coma and his followers and Borodin's faction are eliminating each other."

Kappa felt satisfaction at doing his job well. "Er, you said almost complete success."

"Yes, Kappa. The transplant of Borodin's microbiome into your guts produced some undesirable effects."

Kappa recalled slugging the vodka and the taste of the burger. "You mean I acquired Borodin's taste in food and drink."

"It was a bit more than that, Kappa. You were beginning to acquire his personality too. I've forgiven you for the slap but I'm not so sure of your reference to me as a slut."

Inspired by *A Cloud of Distinction*, by Julian Smith, New Scientist p.39 No.3063, 5/03/2016

A Diet of Treachery – Introduction

This story too was inspired by a New Scientist article. It uses a similar area of science for its inspiration – it's amazing what the gut microbiome can do. This time, Kappa is in trouble.

A Diet of Treachery

Selene Tillington took her seat in front of the armoured glass screen. Beyond it, Agent Kappa slumped in the steel chair screwed to the floor of the small chamber. That a fine agent should have been reduced to this. Selene suppressed a sigh before starting to speak.

"You know why you're here, Kappa. We need answers before we let you rot in prison."

Her words had an effect on the prisoner. He flinched as if pierced by a stiletto, but he did not reply.

She continued, "Your treachery has cost the lives of a dozen agents. Good men and women all of them. Why? How did an agent as highly trained and competent as you, come to betray so many people?"

Kappa raised his head and she saw his face for the first time. The pain was visible in every crease.

His voice came in a slow whisper. "I can't explain it."

"Were you tortured?" Selene asked. She knew the answer. There were no signs of physical injury on his body, not new ones anyway.

The prisoner shook his head. An agent of Kappa's calibre wouldn't have given away so many secrets whatever pain had been inflicted on him. From her previous knowledge of him she would have expected him to die before revealing any vital information.

"Drugs then?" Selene persisted. That too was rhetorical. Medical tests carried out when Kappa has been recovered showed no traces of truth potions or mind-altering drugs other than the chemical signals of the depression that Kappa had undoubtedly sunk into. That must have occurred when he realised the extent of his betrayal.

Kappa shook his head again.

Selene looked at him, disgust a lump in her stomach. Kappa had survived while those he had betrayed died. What was particularly galling was that for all his time in the enemy's hands he looked to be in good health.

"Your captors treated you well," Selene commented. "You weighed more when you were returned to us than when you set off on your mission."

"They looked after me," Kappa admitted with a shrug. "The food was good,"

That was strange, an anomaly, Selene thought. Captured agents were usually put through all sorts of trials to break them: beatings, sleep deprivation, starvation, sexual abuse, mock executions. Simply treating an agent well wouldn't turn them, surely.

"How did they feed you?" she asked.

Kappa's eyebrows rose. He probably hadn't expected this line of questioning.

"Breakfast, lunch, dinner. Regular. It's how I kept track of time."

"No, not the mealtimes. What foods did they give you?"

Kappa looked bemused and then she could see him thinking, remembering.

"Lots of muesli, seeds and grains, with yoghurt; soup, Japanese stuff, miso is it? Dinner was usually something made to look like meat."

"Tofu?"

"No, made with soybeans."

"Ah, tempeh," Selene said, nodding.

"Yeah. There was usually sauerkraut or kimchi, with it."

"It all seems pretty healthy," Selene said. "They were keeping you fit. Why?"

Kappa grunted and subsided into his depressed slouch. The diet sounded unusual to say the least. Something was tickling the grey cells in her skull; something that might answer the questions about Kappa's behaviour. She needed to quiz some of her people.

Just half an hour later, Selene returned to her seat. Kappa had not, apparently, moved.

"We're going to need a stool sample, Kappa," she said.

The agent stirred and for the first time looked at her with something like his old interest.

"You're taking the crap?"

"That's right, Kappa. Those foods the enemy fed you, they're all probiotics. Great for getting bacteria into your gut."

"So, they were concerned for my health," Kappa said.

"Perhaps, but it could be something else."

Kappa's eyebrows rose. She could see he was thinking, looking for connections, explanations. But he couldn't know everything. That's why they kept the research division busy.

Two days later, the senior scientist sat in front of Tillington. She knew him by reputation but not by name.

"I presume you have some results for me," she said.

The man straightened in his seat and took on an air of importance. "Yes, I do. They're interesting. I didn't think the other side were this far advanced in psychobiotics. They've given our work extra impetus."

"I'm glad about that, but how does it affect Agent Kappa?"

"Well, your guess was accurate."

Ah, flattery. A good thing that he knew his place. "In what way?"

"When we spoke, you said that the enemy had been feeding Kappa probiotic foods. You thought that was significant."

Yes, she did, but now he was drawing out his denouement. She would humour him for now.

"How was it significant?"

The man took a deep breath as if about to launch into a lecture. "Probiotics introduce bacteria into the gut microbiome. Usually, the objective is to assist digestion and improve health."

"Not in this case I gather. They weren't particularly interested in keeping Kappa fit and well."

He nodded. "Not really. They were getting some specific bacteria into his system, a tailored strain of *Prevotella* to be precise."

"So what?"

"Once in the intestines they secrete neurotransmitters that give the symptoms of depression and even dementia. In that state the mind becomes suggestible. It wouldn't have taken long for them to persuade Kappa that he was worthless and that the information he held of no importance."

"You mean that they manipulated Kappa's brain, his emotions, his basic mental state through a bunch of bugs in his bowels."

"Yes, Ma'am. It's perfectly feasible. We've been working on the principle for some time. I'm just somewhat surprised that they have a stable and effective strain."

A month later, Selene visited Agent Kappa in his rooms, still in a secure unit but no longer technically a gaol. He looked more like the agent she knew, smartly dressed, hair combed, alert. There was still a deep frown on his face.

"Good morning, Boss. I gather I am no longer accused of betraying my colleagues," he said.

"Technically you were responsible for that Kappa, but now we know you couldn't help it."

"What happened to me?"

"Your, er, sample, showed the presence not only of a highly active *Prevotella* strain but other psycho-biotics. They changed your brain chemistry. I don't quite understand how it works but you literally weren't in your right mind. It took little suggestion by your interrogators to persuade you to divulge the information they wanted."

Kappa shook his head. "I do, kind of, remember how I felt. There was no point to anything, I was useless and unimportant. I couldn't care less about the other agents or what would happen to me."

"That was the effect of the bacteria in your gut."

"But I don't feel that way now."

"No. We fed you antibiotics to kill off everything in your digestive system."

"I had the runs for days."

"Some punishment for your failure, a step in your redemption."

"I feel fine now."

"You should. You received a faecal transplant that has packed you full of good, mind-enhancing psycho-bacteria. The labs tailored special ones just for you. You see we're in an arms race. Our bugs must be better than theirs. You are fit for duty, Kappa, fitter than ever. Now you can avenge your betrayal."

Kappa drew himself tall and erect and gave her that familiar leer, "I've got the guts for it, Boss."

Inspired by: *Psychobiotics: How gut bacteria mess with your mind,* John Cryan and Timothy Dinan, New Scientist, 22 January 2014

P R Ellis, a short biography

I was born and brought up in Cardiff. I enjoyed my school days and showed an aptitude for science. Perhaps that is what switched me on to SF. I read lots and wrote some short stories but did nothing with them. I also enjoyed music, mainly classical then, and learned to pay the piano and church organ badly.

After university in Canterbury, I settled on teaching science, mainly chemistry, as a career. Teaching took me to various parts of southern England where after a period as simply a teacher, I became Head of the Science Department and variously Director of Studies, Head of Sixth Form and Director of Teaching & Learning. I also pursued an interest in the history of science, particularly chemistry. This got me into writing textbooks, or more accurately "educational materials", for various publishers. Writing became my principal career on two occasions. First when I spent four years out of full-time teaching and then when I took early retirement.

While writing non-fiction I also got back into letting my imagination loose but until I retired I gave little thought to publishing my fiction. I did however start attending writing groups and did a one year, one evening a week, course in creative writing at Oxford University Department of External Studies.

During my teaching career I also succeeded in getting married twice. My first to Gill was shortlived but Lou and I have now been married for 35 years. Lou had two children and we now have four marvellous grandchildren.

For decades I have had questions about my gender. It's impossible to say when or how it began but in 2000 I belatedly revealed my feelings to Lou. She has been wonderfully understanding and supportive. My identity has developed in the years since, and I now adopt the terms non-binary and gender fluid to describe myself. I don't really care what pronouns are used but I prefer to avoid the title Mr (or any other for that matter).

A consequence of my "coming out" was a desire to write more fiction. This resulted in five crime novels featuring detective Jasmine Frame, a transwoman going through the stages of transition. They are not autobiographical but, impatient to get the books published, I ended up self-publishing under my own imprint, **ellifont**. The first, *Painted Ladies*, was published in 2013 and the latest, *Impersonator*, in 2021. However, I was also writing fantasy novels and I was delighted to find small publisher, **Elsewhen Press**, willing to take on my efforts. They have currently published five novels, the latest, *An Extraordinary Tale: A Gnome's Odyssey* is just out. There will be a sequel!

Of course, I have also been attending writing groups over the years and this volume, a companion to the earlier collection of SF&F tales, is evidence of the fun I have had with all my writing friends.

In retirement I was keen to get back to Wales. Lou and I now live in Monmouth where we are very happy indeed.

Sept. 2023

Acknowledgements

All the stories in this collection are my own. I have done the editing, proofreading, designing, formatting and uploading, hence all the errors and omissions are my own responsibility. Nevertheless, there are people to thank for helping to get this anthology published. First, and most important to me, is Lou who has read nearly everything I've written (fiction, anyway) in the last 35+ years and has supported me in all my ventures. Then there are the friends who read the early versions of this anthology and given their opinions and advice. By no means least, are all the friends at the writing clubs I have attended over the years who have provided the prompts, listened or read my stories and offered critiques and encouragement. I really do appreciate what a writing group can provide for an author, published or unpublished. Finally, I must thank you the reader for getting this far. Some people write merely for the delight of writing. I, like many others write for the added pleasure of having other people read what I have written. Thank you for being one of those people.

Prompted Visions

An anthology of SF & F tales for writing groups by

P R Ellis

A man lost in a town that has become unfamiliar.
A group of spaceship pilots meet for a celebration.
An aurora spotter experiences a display like no other.

Three of the storylines in this collection of short science fiction and fantasy stories. Each story was written to a prompt and then read out to writing groups of which the author has been a member. A host of different themes, settings, characters and styles. Visit different worlds, times, cultures, and heaven.

Available as an e-book from Amazon Kindle ISBN 978-1-8381935-3-9
and as an Amazon paperback ISBN 978-1-8381935-4-6
Also available from the author, contact
prelliswriter@btinternet.com

Printed in Great Britain
by Amazon

29384883R00096